EST FOR HIDDEN TREASURE

Principles from the Book of Proverbs

Quest for Hidden Treasure: Principles from the Book of Proverbs

Author: Stephen Davey
Editor: Jarl K. Waggoner
Body Layout: Kristin Preston
Cover Design: Kent Perigo
ISBN 978-1-944189-46-4

Published by Charity House Publishers

Charity House Publishers, Inc.
2703 Jones Franklin Road
Suite 105
Cary, NC 27518
USA

www.wisdomonline.org

CONTENTS

1

AS THE CURTAIN RISES

2 Samuel 12 & 2 Chronicles 1

Somewhere east of the city of Flagstaff, Arizona, is the buried loot of a robbery still waiting to be discovered. In 1881, silver and gold coins that would be valued at a million dollars today were stolen when a stagecoach was robbed as it traveled westbound to California. Four canvas mailbags were taken by five masked bandits who surrounded the coach and stole the bags. A few hours later, a posse began the chase and eventually caught up with the outlaws at a spring. In a blazing gunfight, all five outlaws were killed. The entire area was searched and dug up, but despite the efforts of numerous people, the loot was never found.[1]

The lure of hidden treasure has intrigued millions of people the world over. Treasure hunters have formed an entire subculture with group trips and websites and clues regarding sites where buried treasure might yet be found.

In 1968, archaeologists were excavating and cleaning an ancient synagogue in Eshtemoa, in Israel's West Bank area. They also explored a room attached to the synagogue's outer wall, in which a villager had lived until very recently. Less than two feet below the floor of that room, the archaeologists discovered sixty-two pounds of silver that had been stored in earthen jars and buried. Worth tens of thousands of dollars, if not more, it was the largest silver hoard ever discovered in Israel.[2]

Imagine all the former occupants of that room. "If only I had known, I would have dug down, and the treasure would have been mine!" Imagine, living so close to treasure and never knowing it was there.

Here's something else to imagine. You've purchased an old fixer-upper house built in the early 1900s. One Saturday morning as you are cleaning out the attic of your home, you discover an old sheet of paper, yellowed and brittle with age, tacked to a rafter. You carefully take it down and try to open it, but as you unfold it, it falls apart. However, the faded words, "buried treasure" catch your attention.

Your heart begins to beat rapidly as you rush downstairs to the kitchen counter, where you put the pieces of the note together and get out a magnifying glass. You read the words:

> "For some time now, my grown children have given me the impression that they want their inheritance and would really like to be rid of me. Furthermore, I have concluded that my wealth will deepen their greed and ultimately ruin their lives. Therefore, I have decided to bury my money for you—the owner of my humble home. You will find a little more than one million dollars in cash, savings bonds, and gold coins, buried in a small safe in the backyard. Locate the exact middle point of the back property line, walk three paces toward the house, and you will find the safe buried two feet down. I hope you enjoy your inheritance."[3]

After reading that note, would you discard it with the thought, *I'm not falling for that*? Would you tell your neighbor, "Look, I don't have time for a treasure hunt; if you want to dig around out back, you can keep whatever you find"?

You would rush for your property map, grab a tape measure, and race for the backyard in search of this hidden treasure.

As useful as a million dollars could be to you right now, or as exciting as it might be to discover that buried loot near Flagstaff, Arizona, nothing will change your life more than finding the hidden treasure of wisdom offered to us by God Himself. He happens to have left us a note—a collection of clues along the way—to lead us to the places in life where wisdom lies waiting to be discovered and applied.

Solomon tells us in Proverbs 2:4 that we must search for wisdom as for *hidden treasures*. He writes further in Proverbs 3:13-15:

> How blessed is the man who finds wisdom and the man who gains understanding. For her [wisdom's] profit is better than the profit of silver and her gain better than fine gold. She is

more precious than jewels; and nothing you desire compares with her.

You want real treasure? Ransack the treasure map of Scripture to find where wisdom can be found, how it acts, what it looks like, and how to possess it throughout life.

It's one thing to live *rich*; it's another thing to live *right*. It's one thing to make great investments; it's another thing to have great insight. This treasure called wisdom is the difference between someone who knows how to make a living and someone who knows how to make life *worth* living.

Keep in mind that the hidden treasures of wisdom are not for the curious but for the serious.[4] Robert Jeffress tells about seeing on display a Bible that had been given to Albert Einstein. On the flyleaf someone had written, "Straw on the surface flows, but he who searches for pearls must dive below."[5]

Before we start digging for the treasures of wisdom, let's travel back to where the book of Proverbs had its beginning.

SOLOMON'S PREPARATION

Let's begin in the delivery room where Solomon uttered his first cry in 2 Samuel chapter 12.

From the very moment of Solomon's birth, he was surrounded by drama, by royal intrigue. In the approximate twenty-four months prior to his birth, Solomon's father, David the king, had committed adultery and murder. David saw to it that Uriah, the woman's husband, was killed in battle in order to cover up the fact that the baby she was carrying wasn't her husband's child but his. David then married the young widow, Bathsheba.

Insiders knew the real story, and the prophet Nathan eventually exposed the king and his new bride as evil conspirators who had kept terrible secrets. Their baby was soon delivered, but in accordance with Nathan's word, the child died as a sign of God's immediate judgment on David and Bathsheba.

The good news is that David confessed his sin to God. In fact, Psalm 51 records his agonizing and authentic confession and repentance before the Lord.

We have every reason to believe Bathsheba repented as well. In fact, instead of their marital relationship becoming strained by guilt, they conceived another child, and Bathsheba bore the son who would become the heir to the throne of David.

Let's pick up the drama at 2 Samuel 12:24: **Then David comforted his wife Bathsheba, and went in to her and lay with her; and she gave birth to a son, and he named him Solomon.**

Solomon actually had several names, and in the days of the Old Testament, more so than today, names were highly significant. Many parents gave their children names that spoke of qualities they prayed their children would grow up to demonstrate in life.

Solomon, a derivative of the Hebrew word *shalom*, means "peace." David hoped that Solomon would be free from the constant fighting his dad had been involved in and that the kingdom would experience peace under the rule of his son.

The Lord then gave Solomon another name: **Now the LORD loved him and sent word through Nathan the prophet, and he named him Jedidiah for the LORD's sake** (verses 24-25). Jedidiah simply means "loved by the Lord." Many believe the wise prophet, Nathan, became Solomon's tutor and friend.[6]

Can you imagine growing up, hearing that God Himself had given you your middle name and the meaning of that name is "loved by the Lord"? You might think, *Man, if only I had that kind of word from God, that kind of prophetic attention, I would have so few anxious feelings and discouraging times. I would wake up every morning, rain or shine, rich or poor, sick or healthy, and simply remember my name and sail off into whatever the day brings forth.*

Really? We've been given many names—saint, friend, child of God. Aren't they enough to make a difference in our daily lives?

The name Jedidiah didn't make Solomon wake up every day automatically reveling in the grace and goodness and providence of God. He still fought the same battles with temptation and materialism and lust and greed and anger that every believer wages. In fact, sadly, Jedidiah will eventually resign from the fight in disobedience and despair.

Another name that appears in the book of Proverbs is Lemuel. The famous chapter 31 of Proverbs begins with the words, "The words of King Lemuel . . . which his mother taught him."

Lemuel simply means "belonging to God." I agree with those Old Testament scholars who believe Lemuel was another name for Solomon, a name of dedication, by which his mother referred to him even into Solomon's maturing years.

This name was the personal testimony of Bathsheba as she dedicated Solomon to God. She didn't want Solomon to forget it. She had indeed repented and was herself following after God. Additional evidence of this is seen in the fact that Solomon's proverbs repeatedly challenge us to listen, not only to the advice of our fathers, but also to that of our mothers.

Every mother can take heart from the book of Proverbs. You have not been left out; in fact, your counsel is given as much weight as the instruction of a father.

The Message paraphrases Proverbs 6:20-21 as follows:

> Friend, follow your father's good advice; don't wander off from your mother's teachings. Wrap yourself in them from head to foot; wear them like a scarf around your neck. Wherever you walk, they'll guide you; whenever you rest, they'll guard you; when you wake up, they'll tell you what's next. For sound advice is a beacon, good teaching is a light, moral discipline is a life path.

Learn from your father . . . listen to your mother.

What a wonderful, implicit compliment Solomon gives, not only to his father David, but also to his mother Bathsheba—parents with a sordid past. If there is a principle in this for us, it is this: *God's grace can be found at work in the present, in spite of your past.* Godly parenting can still take place in homes that have an ungodly past.

Early on, Solomon would learn that the living God of David and Bathsheba forgives sin and gives new opportunities to follow Him. It was that spirit that Solomon picked up early on in life.

The heart of Solomon is ready to begin a quest for wisdom.

SOLOMON'S DESIRE

Shortly after he succeeded his father as Israel's king, Solomon had a unique encounter with the Lord. It's recorded in 2 Chronicles chapter 1.

God's Offer

While David had brought the ark of the covenant to Jerusalem, the tabernacle and the bronze altar were still at Gibeon, about six miles northwest of Jerusalem.

> **Solomon went up there before the LORD to the bronze altar which was at the tent of meeting, and offered a thousand burnt offerings on it. In that night God appeared to Solomon and said to him, "Ask what I shall give you."** (2 Chronicles 1:6-7)

So, here's the Lord saying, "Make a wish, Solomon. Name it, and it's your coronation gift—from Me to you. What would you like to have?"

Now this sounds about as likely as you finding a note in your attic that buried treasure is out in your backyard. But it *actually* happened to Solomon. In fact, there isn't any indication in our text that Solomon was limited to only one wish. Notice again the Lord's offer: **"Ask what I shall give you."**

Solomon's Response

What's interesting is that Solomon does not immediately express his wish.

He Gives Thanks for What He Has

> **Solomon said to God, "You have dealt with my father David with great lovingkindness, and have made me king in his place."** (2 Chronicles 1:8)

If Solomon had rushed into his first wish, it would have revealed discontent and dissatisfaction. Don't overlook this initial response: "Solomon, what do you wish for?" "Well, Lord, first I want to *thank You for what I have*."

I remember reading of how an American oil company began work in another country. The nationals who worked for this company were relatively poor, but they really didn't know it. Then one day one of the workers happened to see a Sears mail-order catalog in the break room and thumbed through it and then asked if he could take it home. Soon, all the employees had their own catalogs, and every family was eventually in debt and frustrated with the wages they received. They were better off when they did not know how much they did not have. One author wrote, "Contentment is realizing that you are better off the way you are right now."[7]

The mission of advertising is to convince you that you do not have that one thing that you need. You need something else . . . something more . . . something better.

On the other hand, we read this in the book of Proverbs:

> Two things I ask of you, O Lord . . . give me neither poverty nor riches, but feed me the food that is just enough for the daily portion I need. Otherwise, I may have too much and say, "Who needs the Lord?" (Proverbs 30:7-9 paraphrased)

These amazing words appear in Solomon's collection of proverbs—and Solomon was born with the proverbial silver spoon in his mouth. Didn't he *already* have it made?

In the Middle Ages, it was the custom for the godparents of a child to present the child with a silver spoon at his or her christening. From that moment the child could be fed with a special spoon made of silver. However, children born to wealthy parents didn't have to wait to be fed with the finest of utensils; they were born, so to speak, with a silver spoon *already* in their mouth.

This was Solomon, a man who could eat with utensils made of solid gold. It was a splendid kingdom he inherited and reigned over. You might expect him, even as 2 Chronicles opens, to be spoiled and ungrateful. Yet he clearly had developed a sincere and humble gratitude for what the Lord had given him.

He Gives God the Credit for Who He Is

> **"Now, O Lord God, Your promise to my father David is fulfilled, for You have made me king over a people as numerous as the dust of the earth."** (2 Chronicles 1:9)

Gratitude and humility are in the treasure chest where wisdom lives.

First, Solomon gives thanks for what he has; second, he gives the credit to God for who he is. Only then does he make his request.

He Asks God for What He Needs

> **"Give me now wisdom and knowledge, that I may go out and come in before this people, for who can rule this great people of Yours?"** (2 Chronicles 1:10)

When Solomon describes the people he rules as "great," he uses a word that can be rendered "heavy." In essence, he's saying, "Lord, there isn't any way I can bear the heavy burden of this people. I cannot carry the load of responsibility that comes with my crown . . . I need divine assistance!"

Have you ever prayed something like that—"Lord, I can't be the parent, the teacher, the employer, the employee, the student, or the spouse I should be without divine assistance; I need help"? Solomon would be thrilled to hear you pray like that—he knew wisdom comes only to those who know they need it!

The first step in the treasure hunt for wisdom is admitting your need. When you recognize that you lack wisdom, you will ask God for it. He promises to deliver what you need and not rebuke you for asking for it over and over again (James 1:5).

Solomon's unique encounter with the Lord is also recorded in 1 Kings 3. There Solomon's response is worded as a request for an "understanding heart" (verse 9), or literally, a *hearing* heart. This adds an interesting thought to his one wish from God.

What do our hearts hear? What are we listening to? What are our hearts tuned to hear?

In the book of Proverbs, wisdom is pictured as calling out to the passersby, inviting them to embrace her knowledge and discernment. But they pass on without hearing her (Proverbs 1:20-33).

Solomon essentially says to the Lord, "Oh Lord, give my heart the proper antennae; tune my heart to hear from You!" And God grants his wish.

Pastor Ed Young wrote a commentary covering much of Solomon's life entitled, *Been There, Done That: Now What?* In it he tells the story of two men walking together down a crowded sidewalk in Manhattan one afternoon. One of the men was an American Indian, and the other man was a born-and-bred New Yorker. The noise was incredible—cars, buses, horns, sirens, and people talking loudly as they moved down the street.

Suddenly, the Indian said, "Listen, I hear a cricket. Do you hear it?" The New Yorker was incredulous. "No way! You couldn't possibly hear a cricket on a Manhattan sidewalk during rush hour."

"I'm serious," his friend countered. And to prove it, he stopped, bent down, and retrieved a chirping cricket from a crack in the sidewalk.

"How in the world could you hear that?" the New Yorker asked. "Easy," said his friend. "I've lived outdoors most of my life. I can hear a cricket over other noises because my ears are trained to hear those sounds. It's really not that amazing. If you want to see amazing, watch this!" And with those words, he reached into his pocket, pulled out a quarter, flipped it up into the air, and let it drop onto the concrete sidewalk. As soon as it hit the cement, heads began to turn. It seemed as if every New Yorker around heard that coin hit the ground.[8]

Solomon is saying, "Lord, this is my wish: Train my heart to hear the faintest whisper of insight. Tune my heart to the sounds and the ways of wisdom. I want the hidden treasure that makes someone truly rich."

The curtain is about to rise on one of the most remarkable kings of Old Testament times and a young man who would rightly earn the title of "the wisest man who ever lived."

As Solomon collects and composes some three thousand proverbs, he is at his best. When he eventually abandons his search for wisdom, he will be at his worst.

At the outset of our search for wisdom through Proverbs, let me emphasize two important principles.

First, *wisdom is not for those who want it; it is for those who can't live without it.* Simply put, wisdom requires that you begin the hunt with all diligence—as if you were racing out the back door of your home with your tape measure and a shovel and a map.

Second, *wisdom is not for those who are willing to hear about it; it is for those willing to practice it.* The writer of Hebrews describes mature Christians as those who "because of practice have their senses trained to discern good and evil" (Hebrews 5:14). Wisdom seekers learn by practice to discern, or distinguish, differences. They learn to uncover the clues that determine what is good and what is evil.

Under Solomon Israel would see its finest days, for it had a king who made a wish and began a quest for the hidden treasure of wisdom.

When you desire wisdom, and you are willing to pursue it and practice it, you will discover wisdom for life. Solomon should know. From personal experience, he could attest to this promise:

> If you cry for discernment, lift your voice for understanding; if you seek her as silver and search for her as for hidden treasures; then you will discern the fear of the LORD and discover the knowledge of God, for the LORD gives wisdom. (Proverbs 2:3-6)

With that, we're invited to begin a life-fulfilling quest for the treasures that show us how to live life at its highest level and for the greatest good—to the glory of God.

2

WISER THAN AN OWL

Proverbs 1:1-6

Someone sent me this list of "The Perks of Getting Older":

- In a hostage situation, you are likely to be released first.
- People call at 9:00 p.m. and ask apologetically, "Did I wake you?"
- You no longer think of speed limits as a challenge.
- Your investment in health insurance is finally paying off.
- There's nothing left to learn the hard way.
- Your secrets are safe with your friends because they can't remember them either.

Although there are some advantages to getting older, it's another thing to grow wiser.

The book of Psalms tells us how to get along with God. The book of Proverbs tells us how to get along with people. The book of Psalms helps us know how to worship, while the book of Proverbs helps us know how to walk.

The book of Proverbs can be read with one eye on the text and one eye on the daily news. A sentence or two from Proverbs in the middle of a quick lunch break can shape the rest of your day. This inspired collection of *God's* wisdom can help you navigate life in the fast lane.

Derek Kidner wrote of the book of Proverbs:

> It is a book which seldom takes you to church. Like its own figure of Wisdom, it calls across to you in the street about some everyday matter, or points things out at home. Its function in Scripture is to put godliness into working clothes.[1]

Warren Wiersbe wrote that Proverbs is a book that tells you "how to become skillful in the lost art of making a life."[2] This book is filled with the hidden treasures of wisdom—and they are available for any treasure hunter who cares to dig beneath the surface.

WHAT IS A PROVERB?

"The Hebrew word translated 'Proverbs' . . . is derived from the root word *māshāl*, which means 'to rule.'"[3] Thus, a proverb is a rule or principle that gives guidance for wise living.

The English word *proverb* apparently tracks back to the Latin word *proverba*. This is a compound word. *Pro* means "on behalf of," and *verba* means "words." A *proverb*, then, is a short statement on behalf of many words.[4]

Proverbs always have been a key means of teaching great truths simply and quickly. You'll find them in every culture and every generation.

Familiar proverbs include: "Look before you leap," "Nothing ventured, nothing gained," and "Better to be standing on shore wishing you were sailing than sailing wishing you were on shore." Mark Twain provided a proverb that President Harry Truman liked so much he had it framed and hung in the Oval Office: "Always do right—this will gratify some and astonish the rest."[5]

A short saying or proverb I put to memory recently is this one: "You are most likely to hang yourself on the loose threads of life." Here's another one that's worth remembering: "Your silence may be misinterpreted, but it can never be misquoted."

Proverbs summarize deep lessons of truth in a few words. And no proverbs are more important than those recorded in the book of Proverbs, simply because they are the inspired record of Scripture. God, the Giver of wisdom, gave us the book of Proverbs as divine revelation to guide our lives.

Rarely are we given an explicit, written purpose statement from a book of the Bible. The Gospel of John is one of the few cases. There the apostle John wrote these words:

> Therefore many other signs Jesus also performed in the presence of the disciples, which are not written in this book; but *these have been written so that you may believe that Jesus is the*

> *Christ, the Son of God*; and that believing you may have life in His name. (John 20:30-31, italics added)

Solomon, likewise, leaves no question or confusion about his purpose for this Old Testament book of Proverbs. Proverbs 1:1 gives the book what is essentially its title: **The proverbs of Solomon the son of David, king of Israel.** This is followed in the next five verses by the purpose or benefits of the proverbs.

WHAT IS THE PURPOSE OF PROVERBS?

To Know Wisdom

First and foremost, the overarching treasure of Solomon's proverbs is that they cause one **to know wisdom** (verse 2). In other words, Solomon says, "I've given you these proverbs to deliver *to* you and develop *in* you wisdom."

The Hebrew word for **wisdom** is *chokmah*. This is the ability to make the right decision, for the right reason, at the right time. But where does wisdom come from?

The Celtic religions believed their goddess Cerridwen created wisdom. The Romans believed wisdom came from Minerva, and the Hindus point to their goddess of wisdom known as Saraswati.

The Greeks believed wisdom came from the offspring of Zeus. In their mythology, Zeus had heard a prophecy that his wife was going to give birth to a girl who would become the Lord of heaven. Overcome with jealousy, he swallowed his pregnant wife whole. However, when it was time for the child to be delivered, Zeus got a terrible headache, and through an opening in his head, Athena, his daughter stepped out. Because she came from his head, she became the goddess of wisdom. Athens would be named after her. They built the Parthenon in her honor. She was represented by *an owl* as her sacred bird. This gave rise to the superstition that lasts to this day that the owl is a wise bird. We even talk about being wiser than an owl.[6]

The Bible tells us that wisdom comes from God. Romans 16:27 describes Him as "the only wise God." Wisdom is first and foremost a divine attribute. James writes, "If any of you lacks wisdom, let him ask of God, who gives to all generously and without reproach, and it will be given to him"

(James 1:5). Paul's prayer for the Colossians was that they "may be filled with the knowledge of His will in all spiritual wisdom and understanding" (Colossians 1:9).

God communicates His wisdom through the indwelling *presence* of the living Word and the enriching *power* of the written Word. David writes, "The law of the Lord is perfect, restoring the soul; the testimony of the Lord is sure, making wise the simple" (Psalm 19:7). He goes on in verse 8 to write, "The precepts of the Lord are right, rejoicing the heart; the commandment of the Lord is pure, enlightening the eyes."

The written Word of God imparts the ability to make the right decision at the right time for the right reason. Paul reminded Timothy, "You have known the sacred writings which are able to give you the wisdom that leads to salvation through faith which is in Christ Jesus" (2 Timothy 3:15).

In other words, wisdom is developed as a result of hearing and obeying Scripture. The wisest person in the church is not necessarily the *smartest* person but the person who is most *submissive* to the Scriptures.

Solomon's desire is that through the proverbs people will come to know true wisdom.

To Know Instruction

Second, Solomon says in Proverbs 1:2 that another purpose for those who seek the truths presented in Proverbs is that they will **know . . . instruction.** The Hebrew word here (*musar*) carries the idea of a parent's instruction or discipline, which builds character.

Instruction refers to gaining knowledge based not only on hearing the truth but also on learning from the mistakes of others. Solomon promises that by reading this book you can learn from others' experiences.[7]

Have you ever learned something from someone else's mistakes? As a boy, I was convinced that you could jump off the back side of our garage roof—about a ten-foot drop to the grassy backyard—without getting hurt *if* you held an umbrella in your hand. Evidently, I had watched *Mary Poppins* one too many times. I was sure the umbrella would allow you to float down without any problems. Well, I wasn't *totally* certain of my hypothesis, so I convinced my younger brother that it would work. He happily went ahead with it, and as soon as he jumped, the umbrella swooshed inside out and he hit the ground. His experience was highly instructive.

Solomon is going to show us individuals making good decisions and bad ones so that we can be instructed by both.

To Gain Discernment

Solomon goes on in verse 2 to deliver another purpose for the book of Proverbs; namely, that it will help one **to discern the sayings of understanding**. Discernment is the ability to distinguish between opposites: good from evil, right from wrong, honor from dishonor. It is activated by the living Word, through the written Word of God as it is submitted to and lived out.

To Produce Wise Behavior

Solomon adds a fourth purpose—and a fourth treasure—in verse 3. The one who learns Proverbs will **receive instruction in wise behavior.** And what does that wise behavior look like? He tells us: **righteousness, justice and equity.**

Our generation is in desperate need of **wise behavior**.

It's doubtful the statistics have improved any since the mid-1990s, when one author noted that the younger generation was living on the moral edge. He wrote then that every day in America:

- 1,000 unwed teenage girls became mothers
- 1,106 teenage girls had abortions
- 4,219 teenagers contracted a sexually transmitted disease
- 1,000 teens began drinking alcohol
- 500 took their first drugs
- 2,200 teens dropped out of school
- Six committed suicide.[8]

Every day.

The same author wrote:

> The government says the solution is better education; they say more prevention programs will make a better society.

> Educators say the solution is more money; if we pour more money into our schools, we'll produce better kids. Activists say the solution is justice; they contend that we must eradicate injustice and oppression. Others say we need more police, more corporal punishment, more prisons, more job opportunities, more social programs.[9]

These solutions, however, deal only with the *symptoms* of a deeper disease—the lack of wisdom.

To Produce Critical Thinking

Solomon's fifth purpose for collecting Proverbs is **to give prudence to the naive** (verse 4). The Hebrew word for **prudence** can be translated "shrewdness," in the sense of critical thinking.

Why is prudence needed? Because the **naive**, or "simple" as the word is often translated, are inexperienced and gullible. Gullible people believe just about anything, especially something the crowd believes, or something presented by "experts." Proverbs 14:15 says, "The naive believes everything." They're simply "not thinking."[10]

On April 1, 1976, Patrick Moore, a British astronomer, told BBC listeners that very morning the planet Pluto would pass directly behind Jupiter, producing a slight gravitational pull on Earth that momentarily would make everyone weigh less. He urged listeners to jump up and down at precisely 9:47 a.m. and promised they would feel a floating sensation. By 9:48 the switchboards were blazing with delighted callers saying they had experienced the floating sensation when they jumped. One woman said she and eleven friends seated around a table began to float. Another man complained he had risen so rapidly that he hit his head on the ceiling. He wanted compensation for his injury.[11] Leave it to somebody to file a lawsuit.

To Give Guidance

A sixth purpose of this book reveals another benefit for all who learn and practice the proverbs. Proverbs 1:4 says they are recorded to give **to the youth, knowledge and discretion**.

Maybe you're thinking, "Well, that rules me out. I'm not a youth." But the word for **youth** is somewhat elastic; it's used in Scripture to refer to an infant (Exodus 2:6), to a seventeen-year-old (Genesis 37:2), and to a thirty-year-old man (Genesis 41:12). The word seems to refer to anyone on the threshold of maturity. And that fits all of us who are not just growing old but growing *up*.[12]

That's exactly the kind of person Solomon describes in verse 5: **A wise man will hear and increase in learning, and a man of understanding will acquire wise counsel.**

To **acquire** means to grasp or seize. Those who have hands ready to seize and cling to wise counsel find the treasure of wisdom.

To Gain Understanding of Life

Solomon adds one more treasure to his purpose statement by saying that his words will help readers **to understand a proverb and a figure, the words of the wise and their riddles** (Proverbs 1:6).

In Solomon's day, as in every age, people loved riddles. Sophocles, the Greek writer who lived more than four hundred years before the birth of Christ, told the story of Oedipus, who became king of Thebes after solving the riddle of the sphinx. The sphinx, which had the body of a lion, the wings of an eagle, and the head of a woman, guarded the city of Thebes and asked anyone who approached a riddle. Those who could not solve the riddle were killed. The riddle was this: "What has one voice, and yet is four-footed in the morning, two-footed at noon, and three-footed in the evening?" Oedipus gave the correct answer: a human being. As an infant—"in the morning"—a person crawls on all fours. Later in life, he stands on two feet. In the evening of his life, he uses a crutch.[13]

Frankly, life can be a riddle at times. Solomon promises that his collection of proverbs will serve us well. In other words, if you want to figure out the riddles life brings you—some innocent and some far more serious—you need to understand the proverbs written in this book.

According to God's word through Solomon, people who are wise don't know everything, but they long to learn more. They may not know what to say, but they're ready to listen.

Do you want to do more than grow old? Do you want to grow wiser than an owl? This book of Proverbs is the answer. So, let's get ready to listen . . . learn . . . obey.

3

WALKING WISELY IN A WORLD OF FOOLS

Proverbs 1:7

In the preface of Robert Alden's commentary on the book of Proverbs, Haddon Robinson writes these words:

> Since 1955 knowledge has doubled every five years. . . . our generation possesses more data about the universe and human personality than all previous generations put together. High school graduates today have been exposed to more information about the world than Plato, Aristotle, Spinoza, or Benjamin Franklin. In terms of facts alone, neither Moses nor Paul could pass a college entrance exam today.[1]

What I find especially ironic is that much of this quote is now terribly out of date. He wrote this in 1983, and he is now way behind on his facts. Some have even projected that human knowledge will soon be doubling every *twelve hours*! Whether we ever reach that point is yet to be known, but certainly knowledge is increasing at an extremely rapid rate.

Imagine an education that prepares students to hold jobs that haven't been created yet, to use technologies that haven't been invented yet, in order to solve problems that don't currently exist. How do we prepare for a future when we have no idea what it looks like? How do we equip ourselves and our children to handle temptations and pressures that were inconceivable a few decades ago?

With all our expanding knowledge, the world still is not a better place to live. The only thing that's changed is the speed of change . . . and the equipment.

Robinson observed, "Alumni from noted universities have mastered information about a narrow slice of life but couldn't make it out of the first grade when it comes to living successfully with family and friends."[2] He described society as "a bumper crop of brilliant failures."[3]

The truth is, knowledge is not enough. Even if knowledge doubled every two hours, the world would still be full of educated disasters. And while the culture of human experience may change rapidly, the condition of the human heart does not. Paul wrote to Timothy that the world of unbelievers is "always learning and never able to come to the knowledge of the truth" (2 Timothy 3:7).

There must be more to life than knowledge. Facts alone do not provide a foundation for life. That is the issue the book of Proverbs addresses.

Proverbs 1:7 provides the answer as Solomon delivers the key verse in his entire collection:

> **The fear of the Lord is the beginning of knowledge; fools despise wisdom and instruction.**

Knowledge and **wisdom** and **instruction** are synonyms in this context, as Solomon sets forth the premise of Proverbs. They allow a person to make the right decision for the right reason at the right time and apply it in the right spirit, guided by a relationship with God.

Like many of the proverbs, this verse sets forth a contrast. Here the contrast is between the one who fears the Lord and gains knowledge and the one who rejects wisdom and instruction.

THE FOOL

Biblically speaking, fools aren't the slowest people in science class. They are identified in Scripture as disbelieving in God and disregarding His word. They effectively despise **knowledge**, **wisdom**, and **instruction**, as verse 7 says. A fool then is unable to make the *right* decision for the *right* reason at the *right* time and apply it in the *right* spirit in order to attain the *right* effect.

The particular word for **fools** here is used some twenty-six times in the Old Testament, and all but seven of them are found in the book of Proverbs.

The fool is described in living color throughout this book:

- *The fool is unaccountable.* Solomon writes, "The way of a fool is right in his own eyes, but a wise man is he who listens to counsel" (Proverbs 12:15).
- *The fool is unruly.* As Solomon says, "A fool's anger is known at once, but a prudent man conceals dishonor" (Proverbs 12:16). In other words, the wise person holds back his dishonorable feelings; the fool does not.
- *The fool is unteachable.* "A fool rejects his father's discipline [or training], but he who regards reproof is sensible," Solomon writes in Proverbs 15:5. And Proverbs 26:11 says, "Like a dog that returns to its vomit is a fool who repeats his folly." He just won't learn. The fool cannot imagine himself being mistaken. But the root of his problem is not mental; it is spiritual.
- *The fool is unfriendly.* Proverbs 20:3 says, "Keeping away from strife [literally, ceasing from strife] is an honor for a man, but any fool will quarrel." Most people will consider it honorable to stop an argument, but the fool loves to argue for argument's sake.
- *The fool is incorrigible.* There is an incurable element to his foolishness since he denies the existence of God, who alone can rescue him. The fool persists in loving his arrogant self-view and sinful lifestyle. Solomon says, "Though you pound a fool in a mortar with a pestle along with crushed grain, yet his foolishness will not depart from him" (Proverbs 27:22).

Sometimes you shake your head over the foolishness of people. I found a couple news items that illustrate foolishness that you probably couldn't pound out of these people.

> Amy Brasher was arrested in San Antonio, Texas, after a mechanic reported to police that 18 packages of marijuana were packed in the engine compartment of the car which she had brought to the mechanic for an oil change. According to police, Brasher later said that she didn't

> realize that the mechanic would have to raise the hood to change the oil.
>
> A man walked into Burger King in Ypsilanti, Michigan at 7:50 am, flashed a gun and demanded cash. The clerk turned him down because he said he couldn't open the cash register without a food order. When the man ordered onion rings, the clerk said they weren't available for breakfast. The man, frustrated, walked away.[4]

The Message paraphrases Proverbs 27:22 very simply, "Pound on a fool all you want—you can't pound out foolishness." Why is this? Because at the heart of the issue is an unredeemed person. He has chosen his foolishness.

- The fool is unholy. David wrote earlier, "The fool has said in his heart, 'There is no God'" (Psalm 14:1). And as a character in Dostoevsky's novel *The Brothers Karamazov* said, "If God does not exist, everything is permitted."

  That's why Proverbs 14:9 tells us "fools mock at sin," or, as it can be translated, "fools mock at guilt." They are committed to unholy living. They mock moral absolutes. They say your guilt over sin is simply the residue of the Victorian era—too much religion; just shrug it off.

These characteristics explain why brilliant engineers and doctors and mechanics and schoolteachers can be utterly devoid of common sense, utterly incapable of selfless relationships, and utterly wayward in moral attitudes and actions.

Their minds are closed to God, their consciences are seared by sin, and their hearts are fully devoted to themselves.

THE WISE PERSON

Understanding the Fear of the Lord

The wise person, on the other hand, is the one who fears the Lord. Solomon put it this way in Proverbs 1:7: **The fear of the Lord is the beginning of knowledge.**

The Hebrew word translated **beginning** is used fifty times elsewhere and can be understood as something that is *foundational* or *superior*. The principal meaning of the root word is "head," which suggests that which is first or primary.

One Old Testament scholar wrote that fearing the Lord isn't merely a starting point but "a foundation to build upon."[5] The foundation of all true knowledge is a relationship of respect and surrender to God.

In Proverbs 9:10, Solomon repeats the thought, saying it a little differently: "The fear of the Lord is the beginning of wisdom, and the knowledge of the Holy One is understanding." Again, the ability to make the right decision at the right time in the right spirit for the right reason to achieve the right effect derives from a relationship with the creator God. **The fear of the Lord is the beginning**—the foundation—**of knowledge.**

Since fearing the Lord is the beginning of knowledge, we need to understand this compound expression. You cannot determine its meaning simply by separating the two ideas and studying the words *fear* and then *Yahweh* (Lord) separately.

That would be like defining the word *butterfly* by analyzing the words *butter* and *fly* separately.[6] You would end up with an insect that melts in the sun.

Certainly, "fearing God" is a biblical concept. And everyone you read about who gets a glimpse of God's full glory usually faints with fear.

Upon seeing a vision of God, Isaiah cried, "Woe is me, for I am ruined." (Isaiah 6:5). The apostle John saw a vision of God the Son in His glory and "fell at His feet like a dead man" (Revelation 1:17). Even Daniel, after seeing the vision of an exalted visitor, who may well have been Christ, began to tremble uncontrollably and had no strength (Daniel 10:10-17).

Is Solomon suggesting that a wise person walks around in dread of God? Or, is this fear a worshipful reverence that acknowledges the sovereignty of God?[7] If we allow the Bible to interpret the Bible, this phrase is explained and expanded throughout Scripture.

Let me summarize with three characteristics found in someone who fears the Lord.

First, there is joyful delight in the Word of God. The psalmist wrote, "How blessed is the man who fears the Lord, who greatly delights in His commandments" (Psalm 112:1). Psalm 119:103 says, "How sweet are Your words to my taste! Yes, sweeter than honey to my mouth!"

Second, there is a passionate desire to apply the Word of God. We read in Psalm 128:1, "Blessed is everyone who fears the LORD, who walks in His ways." Solomon spells it out even more clearly in Proverbs 14:2: "He who walks in his uprightness fears the LORD, but he who is devious in his ways despises Him."

Third, there is confidence in the promises of God. Psalm 147:11 declares, "The LORD favors those who fear Him, those who wait for His lovingkindness."

These are the characteristics of those who fear the Lord. These, along with the reactions of biblical characters to God's revealed glory, suggest that the fear of the Lord is not paralyzing terror but a deep, worshipful reverence and respect for God that results in true humility and an intimate, trusting, joyful relationship with Him.

Developing the Fear of the Lord

How do you *develop* the fear of the Lord in order to walk wisely in a world of fools? There are several necessary elements in the developmental process.

Through the Word

The fear of the Lord is developed, first, through constant exposure to the Word of God. That should be obvious, right? If the fear of the Lord is evidenced by the study and application of the Word of God, then the way to develop greater fear of the Lord is to study the Word even more.

Look at Psalm 119:38: "Establish [confirm] Your word to Your Servant, as that which produces reverence [fear] for You." The fear of the Lord comes through a relationship with the written Word and the living Word.

A wise person is someone who knows *where* to take his questions regarding relationships, integrity, communication, honesty, purity—namely, to God's Word!

Through Prayer

The fear of the Lord is further developed in our lives through prayer—the kind of prayer offered by the psalmist:

> God, teach me lessons for living so I can stay the course. Give me insight so I can do what you tell me—my whole life one long, obedient response. Guide me down the road of your commandments; I love traveling this freeway! Give me an appetite for your words of wisdom, and not for piling up loot. Divert my eyes from toys and trinkets, invigorate me on the pilgrim way. Affirm your promises to me—promises made to all who fear you. Deflect the harsh words of my critics—but what you say is always so good. See how hungry I am for your counsel; preserve my life through your righteous ways! (Psalm 119:33-40 MSG)

This is the kind of prayer that will help you swim in this ocean of change and multiplying information, while surrounded by fools.

Through Wise Counsel

The fear of God is also developed through listening to the wise counsel of others, such as parents, peers, friends, and mentors. Indeed, "in abundance of counselors there is victory" (Proverbs 11:14). A wise person, according to the Bible, admits he or she doesn't have all the answers.

Chuck Yeager, the famous test pilot, tells of flying the F-86 Sabre jet fighter after several pilots had died in crashes of the Sabre.

> I flew a Sabre as a chase airplane. One day, I flew up into the Sierras to check on a favorite fishing lake. A buddy of mine . . . lived at the edge of the lake, and I came across low to buzz his place, did a slow roll over his house, when suddenly my aileron locked. It was a hairy moment, flying about 150 feet off the ground and upside down. But the moment I let off on the Gs, pushing up the nose, the aileron unlocked. Very strange. I climbed to 15,000 feet, where it was safer to try it again, and each time I performed that rolling maneuver, the aileron locked. I figured that somehow the wings were bending under stress and locking the aileron. I called General Boyd as soon as I landed and told him I thought I knew how those crashes occurred, but not why.

> The old man sent inspectors to take apart my Sabre's wings. They found that a bolt on the aileron cylinder was installed upside down. Crew chiefs in every Sabre squadron were ordered to inspect their airplanes' wings for that upside-down bolt, while an inspection team went to the North American plant and found the culprit. He was an older man on the assembly line who ignored instructions about how to insert that bolt because . . . he knew that bolts were supposed to be placed head up, not head down. Nobody told him how many pilots he had killed.[8]

What a tragically foolish man.

A wise person admits, "Lord, give me the directions. I don't know better than You."

How do you navigate your way through today's vast maze of information—and change? How do you walk with wisdom in a world of fools?

The foundation, the primary thing, is not having all the answers but having an open, honest, committed relationship with your Redeemer—fearing the Lord.

So, even when technology changes rapidly and the world is unsettled around you, cling with reverence and respect to the Rock; passionately apply His revelation, and rejoice in the promises and assurance of His redemption.

And with that, you're ready to walk wisely in a world of fools.

4

BIRDS OF A FEATHER

Proverbs 1:8-19

It's hard for many of us to imagine, but for young people today, the 1990s is ancient history. Rotary phones and typewriters are hardly recognizable. They have never known a world without computers and the internet. Writing a handwritten letter and sending it by mail is almost unheard of. Technological advances, especially in communication, certainly have changed our lives.

Fallen human nature, however, has *not* changed. Indeed, it is expanding its dominance of our culture through the very innovations in communication from which we all profit. For all the information available to us, the truth is often hard to come by, hidden by a multitude of voices declaring their own "truth" and demanding conformity to it. Through social media, the peer pressure that teens and adults alike have always faced has now multiplied, as have the consequences for standing against the cultural tide.

The influence of culture is profound, but culture isn't the problem, which is why the Bible never tells believers to abandon culture and go live in the woods. Rather, the Bible challenges Christians to influence their culture with the gospel while at the same time resisting the gravitational pull of sin.

You've heard the expression, "Birds of a feather flock together." That's not only a fact of nature; it is a fact of *human* nature.

The people with whom you choose to flock will influence you one way or another. Friendship and fellowship with the right people are critically important.

C. S. Lewis called friendship either a school of virtue or a school of vice. He wrote, "It makes good men better and bad men worse."[1]

One of the first things Solomon teaches us is to avoid bad people. You might think that sounds harsh, but it's biblically wise. There are certain flocks to avoid and one flock of birds worth joining.

AVOIDING THE WRONG FLOCK

Having urged obedience to one's parents in Proverbs 1:8, Solomon offers this first fatherly piece of advice:

> **My son, if sinners entice you, do not consent. If they say, "Come with us, let us lie in wait for blood, let us ambush the innocent without cause; let us swallow them alive like Sheol, even whole, as those who go down to the pit; we will find all kinds of precious wealth, we will fill our houses with spoil; throw in your lot with us, we shall all have one purse," my son, do not walk in the way with them. Keep your feet from their path.** (Proverbs 1:10-15)

The word for **sinners** is *hattaim*, which refers in general to those who are missing the mark, those who have fallen short of God's standard. The Hebrew text indicates that sinning is the repeated action of these people.[2]

They aren't sinning and stopping, sinning and repenting. This is their occupation. They are practitioners—experienced veterans—of sinful lifestyles.

Note here that the sinners issue an invitation: **"Come with us."** "You don't have to be like us. You don't have to change your beliefs or even your morals. Just come join us." Solomon advises two responses.

A Verbal Response

The first response is verbal. **Do not consent** is another way of instructing us to say no.

One of the best ways to avoid sin is to say *no* as early as possible. The time to say no to a guy's advances is not at eleven o'clock at night parked by the lake; it's at two o'clock in the afternoon when he asks you out. Say no *then*, and you will never have to say no *there*.

You might be convinced you will say no to embezzlement or adultery, but are you currently cheating on the internet and on your taxes? The time to say no is at the first invitation to sin.

Daniel provides an incredible example for the believer. He was introduced into a new and corrupt culture. He was inducted into the educational system, the leadership training program, of Babylon. The names of Daniel and his friends were even changed to Babylonian names.

- Daniel, which means "God is my judge," was changed to Belteshazzar, which means "Prince of Bel," one of Babylon's chief gods.
- Hananiah, which means "God is gracious," was changed to Shadrach, which means "commanded by Aku (their moon god)."
- Mishael, which means "Who is like God?" was changed to Meshach, which boasts, "Who is like Aku?"
- And Azariah, which means "the Lord is my help," was now Abed-nego, which means "the servant of Nego," the god of fire.

This was all part of the psychological game the Babylonians were playing in an attempt to change the mindset of Daniel and his friends from Judaism to paganism.

Daniel never said no to the educational system of Babylon; in fact, he excelled in it. Neither did he resist his name change, even though he would never consider himself Bel's prince. He never complained about his pagan professors either.

What he did refuse to go along with was the *one thing* that would have caused him to commit sin. Daniel 1:8 informs us that "Daniel made up his mind that he would not defile himself [that is, he would not sin] with the king's choice food or with the wine which he drank."

Israelites were not vegetarians, and they drank wine. So, the only way this meat would defile Daniel is if it were from an unclean animal according to the law of Moses. And if the wine had been offered as a libation to a pagan god—the custom of Babylonian kings—it could have tacitly endorsed idolatry. Daniel's refusal was firm but gracious.

That one little word *no* may save you from a life of regret.

A Physical Response

The second response to sinners who want us to join them is **Do not walk in the way with them. Keep your feet from their path.** Verse 15 provides the proper physical response to the enticement of sinners—namely, stay away!

Solomon continues:

> **For their feet run to evil and they hasten to shed blood. Indeed, it is useless to spread the baited net in the sight of any bird; but they lie in wait for their own blood; they ambush their own lives. So are the ways of everyone who gains by violence; it takes away the life of its possessors.** (verses 16-19)

Here is fatherly advice to a son to consider *the end* of the sinner's path. Sinners may have plenty of friends, live exciting lives, and have money to spend on the weekends. But in the end, they experience emptiness and loss.

Someone is sure to say, "But didn't Jesus Christ make friends with sinners? Wasn't He condemned for eating and drinking with tax collectors and sinners?" True enough; He was (Matthew 11:19).

But Christ had a purpose in mind; He wasn't eating with tax collectors because He was lonely. He wasn't eating with wayward men and women so He could have some friends to party with on the weekend.

He wasn't mingling with them so that they could influence *Him* but so that He could influence *them*—not because He needed them but because they needed Him. He had come to seek and to save those who were lost (Luke 19:10). Jesus wasn't there to entertain them but to redeem them.

Think of friendships or influences in your life as encompassing three concentric circles surrounding you right now. The circle farthest out from you represents *passive acquaintances*. These are kids who sit in your science class or ride the bus home with you. These are the people who work in cubicles next to you. You share the same water fountain and elevator. You know the name of that receptionist and bank manager, and they know yours, but that's as far as it goes. You know them, but you don't know much about them.

The next circle, a bit closer to you, represents *casual friendships*. These are the guys you play with on the soccer team; they not only sit on the same bus as you do, but they also share a seat with you, and you enjoy talking to them as you ride to the game.

These are the people who serve in the same boardroom with you as you hammer out strategic initiatives. These are your neighbors you chat with and invite over on Saturday afternoon. These are the people you talk with in the hallway at school or work. They are much more than acquaintances. In fact, they are pretty much locked into your sphere of living—traveling in the same traffic pattern through life.

You invite them to church. You strike up meaningful conversations with them about Christ. These are the people on your prayer list. Like Christ, you're not spending time with them so that they can influence you; *you* intend to influence them. These are people God has placed in your world so that you can reach them with the gospel.

The third circle, the one closest to you, represents your *close companions*. These are the people you allow into your life to *share* your life. They are your counselors and confidants. You are fortunate to have one or two that you can call close friends.

To these people you have given the right of influence and direction. These are the people you ask, "What do you think I ought to do? Which decision do you think I should make?"

These are the ones who impact your heart and life. This is your flock of birds. They contribute greatly to your life, and you have the opportunity to contribute in some measure to theirs.

As a believer, you should allow *no one* who is without Christ to gain access to this inner circle of influence.

> Thorns and snares are in the way of the perverse; he who guards himself will be far from them. (Proverbs 22:5)

> Do not be bound together with unbelievers; for what partnership have righteousness and lawlessness, or what fellowship has light with darkness? (2 Corinthians 6:14)

If you are dating an unbeliever, or a so-called believer who doesn't care about the things of God, you are granting access to the wrong influence. If your counselor or psychologist or confidant at work doesn't know Jesus Christ, that person should not be granted inner-circle access to influence your mindset.

Perhaps the very best thing you can do for your spiritual walk is to start avoiding certain people. Graciously move someone from your inner circle to an outer circle.

Solomon promised in Proverbs 13:20, "He who walks with wise men will be wise, but the companion of fools will suffer harm." Remember, the word *fool* has nothing to do with someone's SAT scores. A fool throughout Scripture is someone who has said in his heart, "There is no God." Fools deny spiritual authority in heaven and biblical authority on earth.

Don't be fooled by a fool. There are a lot of fools who come to church. They say they believe in God. They sing and testify of their belief in God, but in their hearts, they are "practical atheists." That is, while they say there is a God, in practice they live as if He doesn't exist. That's why David did *not* say, "The fool has said with his *lips*, 'There is no God'" but rather, "The fool has said in his *heart*, 'There is no God'" (Psalm 14:1).

"The companion of fools will suffer harm," Solomon wrote. Bruce Waltke defined a "companion of fools" as someone who allows a fool to shape him "by exciting his interests, forming his resolutions, and fixing his habits."[3] Whom have you allowed to excite your interests, help form your resolutions, and determine your habits? If it's a wise person, you're soaring in the right flock. If it's a fool, you're flying into disaster. Here's how Solomon put it in Proverbs 12:26: "The righteous is a guide to his neighbor, but the way of the wicked leads them astray."

Note the progression of sin presented here in Proverbs 1. It begins in verse 11 with the invitation of the wicked, which leads to a call for participation, and then to cooperation in verse 14.

Invitation . . . participation . . . cooperation.

Where in this process is it the hardest to flee from the wrong flock? Clearly, it's when you are fully cooperating and your heart has become involved.

When is it the easiest to protect that inner circle around you? In the beginning. So, when the invitation arrives, give a simple response: "No, thanks."

FINDING THE RIGHT FLOCK

The question remains: How do you spot a wise flock of birds? Two key characteristics identify wise birds of a feather.

They Believe in the Crucified and Resurrected Christ

Paul wrote in 1 Corinthians 1:23-24:

> We preach Christ crucified, to Jews a stumbling block and to Gentiles foolishness, but to those who are the called, both Jews and Greeks, Christ the power of God and the wisdom of God.

The person who believes that Christ is the epitome of wisdom *is* a wise person. The person who seeks Christ for counsel and guidance, the person who believes Christ is the living, ascended Lord, *is* a wise person. Fly with birds like that!

They Base Their Lifestyle on the Word of Christ

In Matthew 7:24 Jesus Christ said, "Therefore everyone who hears these words of Mine and acts on them, may be compared to a wise man who built his house on the rock." The person who says, "Hey, don't take the Bible so seriously" is not wise. But the person who says, "I have to know what Christ has to say about that" is wise indeed. He will stand against the undertow of sin.

Isn't it interesting that at the outset of the book of Proverbs, the first piece of advice Solomon offers his son is to avoid the wrong people? Solomon is saying, "Son, look all the way down the path, and note how sinners end up. They are heading for ruin and destruction. But you will be kept safe if you avoid them."

Avoiding them might be awkward. It may mean you spend weekends alone. It might mean you're the odd man out at the office. It might mean you're the least likely to be asked out on a date. But you will be delivered from an empty life and the tragic consequences of following fools.

In 1942, Boston College's undefeated football team was considered one of the best in the nation. The season was coming to a close with their homecoming game against lightly regarded Holy Cross, which had lost as many games as they had won that year. All the celebrations and presentations following the game were planned—all the things you want to do at the homecoming party when everyone is feeling good after a victory.

But the victory never came. In that particular game, everything Boston College did went wrong, and everything Holy Cross did went right. At the end of the game, the score was an embarrassing 55 to 12. The Boston College team was so embarrassed that they canceled their big homecoming celebration. They fully expected to wake up the next morning to the headlines, "Boston College Routed by Holy Cross."

However, the next morning, the local newspaper was dominated by another story. A fire had broken out in the Coconut Grove nightclub, taking the lives of almost five hundred people in one of the deadliest fires in American history.

To most people, Boston's College's loss on the football field now seemed very insignificant. But to every player and coach and friend of the Boston College football team, it meant everything. You see, their homecoming celebration had been planned to take place at the Coconut Grove. Their humiliation . . . their embarrassment . . . their emotional pain . . . ultimately had saved their lives.

Sounds like encouragement from Solomon. While it might be embarrassing, difficult, and painfully lonely at times, avoiding the wrong people just might save you from disaster.

Don't fly with the wrong flock of birds. Resist enticement, refuse entanglement, and guard the access points of influence. It will make all the difference, not only in this world but also in the world to come.

5

OBSERVATIONS FROM AN ANTHILL

Proverbs 6:6-11 and Selected Proverbs

There is a vast difference between being tired *from* work and being tired *of* work. In today's world, a good testimony for Christ is found in someone who actually works hard enough to *get* tired.

The average person in America gets paid for forty hours of work per week but actually works thirty. Sick days are always used up, as well as personal days, to go along with vacation days, and holidays. Few of us have ever heard someone ask the boss for added assignments and more difficult tasks.

Don't misunderstand; the Bible doesn't recommend that Christians become workaholics. In fact, the *quantity* of work hours on the job isn't as much of an issue in Scripture as the *quality* of work done.

Paul told the Colossian believers exactly how they were to show up and work on the job. He writes, "Do your work heartily, as for the Lord rather than for men, knowing that from the Lord you will receive the reward . . . it is the Lord Christ whom you serve" (Colossians 3:23-24).

The word Paul uses for "work" refers to work that is done *energetically* or *diligently*.[1] To work "heartily" is literally "out of the soul." In other words, Paul urges believers to put their whole being into their work.

Unfortunately, we've drawn an artificial line between secular and sacred work. We get excited about discipling a group of men but don't sense any divine purpose in doing laundry, laying tile, or filing a brief. We easily forget that we're not working for man but, for the Lord.

The Latin word *vocatio*, which gives us our word *vocation*, means "calling." Your employment, whatever it may be, happens to be God's calling. Your profession is a "pulpit"—a sacred calling through which you honor

Him. Solomon writes, "Whatever your hand finds to do, do it with all your might" (Ecclesiastes 9:10).

Solomon has a lot to say about our *work,* and much of what he says is presented in contrast to the *sluggard*, or lazy person.

THE SLUGGARD DESCRIBED

Throughout the book of Proverbs, Solomon warns his son about the sluggard—the kind of employee no one wants to hire, the worst college roommate you could ever have, the most discouraging player on the team, and the most difficult person to work around. Solomon describes the sluggard with frank language throughout Proverbs, where the word appears a dozen times.

Undependable Patterns

The sluggard's work patterns are undependable. In Proverbs 10:26, Solomon writes, **Like vinegar to the teeth and smoke to the eyes, so is the lazy one to those who send him.**

You can't depend on a lazy person. Give him a deadline, and you will be disappointed. Giving a sluggard a message to deliver will lead you to grind your teeth with frustration over his failure to fulfill that simple task.

Solomon says he is like **smoke to the eyes.** When smoke from a campfire or backyard grill shifts in the wind and blows into your face, your eyes burn from the stinging irritation.

And here's the point: sluggards don't really care. As Bruce Waltke says, they are "without a moral sense of responsibility to others."[2] The boss can only bang his head against the wall, take some medicine for ulcers, and cry tears of frustration.

Unbelievable Excuses

Solomon writes, **The sluggard says, "There is a lion outside; I will be killed in the streets!"** (Proverbs 22:13). This goes beyond calling in sick. That's too simple; "Haven't you heard? There's a lion on the loose!"

It *could* be true, but for the most part, his excuses are so unbelievable you have no idea how to respond. "It's as if the sluggard summons all of his creative energy into making excuses rather than making a living."[3]

Then again, all sluggards are not equally creative. I heard on the news recently of an employee who called his boss, asking if he could miss work to attend his grandmother's funeral. He was given the time off. Six months later he called to get time off for another funeral—his grandmother's. He even used the same grandmother's name. It seems that she had died all over again.

Creative or not, excuses are often nothing more than lies. Believers who are dedicated to professing the glory of God through their vocation will tell the truth—and live the truth at work. Benjamin Franklin once said, "He that is good at making excuses is seldom good at anything else."[4]

Unteachable Spirit

The spirit of a sluggard is unteachable. Proverbs 26:16 says, **The sluggard is wiser in his own eyes than seven men who can give a discreet answer.** Confront those lazy employees about their careless work, late appearances, or failure to meet deadlines, and they'll have a list of defenses. They will essentially refuse any negative review.

Just ask them, and they'll tell you. They're your best employees; they work the hardest; they deserve the most credit and the largest bonuses.

Sluggards will tell you they are wiser and more valuable than anyone else. The truth is, they are costly to their employers. Coworkers have to pull them along. Sluggards can talk, but they simply don't work.

Unreasonable Expectations

Another characteristic of people who are all talk and no work is their unreasonable expectations.

They are the ones who insist they should receive pay raises, accolades, and awards.

They have high expectations. They're going places. You'll see. But watch their lives, and you will discover that in reality they're expecting everything to happen without lifting a finger.

In Proverbs 12:27, Solomon says, **A lazy man does not roast his prey**. If the sluggard finally moves himself to go out to hunt wild game, he never prepares it for supper. He simply can't finish the task.

He's got big plans and dreams and desires, but he's the same guy who says, "Hey, the boss is gone; let's kick back and relax. Let's take a few short-cuts. Don't work so hard."

In chapter 21 we find perhaps the bluntest terms yet regarding the misguided, self-deceived, self-centered arrogance of sluggards: **The desire of the sluggard puts him to death . . . all day long he is craving** (verses 25-26). Literally, he "desires a desire." In other words, every day he wakes up and finally gets out of bed and desires another desire—he covets greatly.[5]

Unaccountable Private Life

Solomon writes in Proverbs 26:14, **As the door turns on its hinges, so does the sluggard on his bed.** Solomon pictures a double-hinged door. There's a lot of movement, turning back and forth, but never any forward motion.[6]

In verse 15 Solomon writes that the sluggard is so lazy that he **buries his hand in the dish** but is too weary to bring the food to his mouth again. This describes total apathy. Even when he's at the table, he doesn't have the initiative to feed himself properly. This person—whether employee, roommate, coworker, or otherwise—is self-destructive.

Proverbs chapter 6 further describes the life of a sluggard behind closed doors as being one of undisciplined laziness. Solomon writes in verse 9, **How long will you lie down, O sluggard? When will you arise from your sleep?** Then in verse 11: **Your poverty will come in like a vagabond and your need like an armed man.**

The sluggard is being robbed of an excellent life and doesn't realize the thief has moved into the guest room and made himself at home. He's not just cutting corners at work—coming in late, making up excuses, not fulfilling his contract—he's allowing his life to be stolen away.

A little sleep, a little slumber, says the sluggard in verse 10. "That's all I'm doing—just taking a nap." Solomon isn't referring to a nap brought on by fatigue through hard work. This is the nap of someone who is too lazy to work. Minute by minute, inch by inch, the sluggard wastes life away by degrees.[7]

THE SOLUTION PROVIDED

There is a solution for the sluggard. Solomon suggests taking a field trip to an anthill. **Go to the ant, O sluggard, observe her ways and be wise.** (Proverbs 6:6)

When our children were young, we purchased a small ant farm—a plexiglass aquarium filled with sand and a bunch of ants. We watched the ants work, digging amazing little tunnels and storing food. Solomon said they are worth studying.

Ants Are Diligent and Organized

Ants are diligent. Their work never ends, and they never stop. Soldier ants guard the colony, and worker ants either clean, care for the queen ant, or gather food—all coded into their created instincts by their creator God.

Some ants keep herds of "cows," which are plant lice. The Mediterranean ant makes "biscuits" from seeds; and honey ants store their food in living storage tanks. Ants have very complex organizations, building projects, and communication systems.[8]

The strongest ants can lift fifty times their body weight.[9] If we possessed that kind of strength, we could pick up the nearest SUV . . . with a full tank of gas.

Leafcutter ants build mounds that contain more than a thousand chambers and house millions of ants.[10] Red fire ants live very organized lives—extremely clean and constantly cleaning the mound.[11] There are some moms who probably wish their kids had some fire ant DNA.

It would be hard to find a more industrious creature on earth.

Ants Are Self-motivated

In verse 7, Solomon notes something surprising: Ants have **no chief, officer or ruler**. Imagine your home state surviving without police officers, government officials, and civil support systems. While ants are organized, no ant organizes them.

One woman described what happened when she visited her parents' home on the farm. Her five-year-old niece had come along, and she joined in picking and shucking corn by hand. At first, the work was great fun, but after a few minutes, this little five-year-old looked up at her grandmother and said, "You know you can buy this in the store, don't you?"[12]

Take your kids to the local strawberry patch to pick their own strawberries, and count the minutes before it is no longer fun.

Ants work tirelessly and are entirely self-motivated. Solomon says in verse 7 that they do it all without a **chief**. The word can be translated "judge." Ants have no need to settle a dispute; they simply move around and over each other. The task is more important than anything else.

This word **chief** can also carry the nuance of a guide. Imagine a mound with thousands of ants and no traffic signals.

Solomon also mentions that ants do not need an **officer**. This word refers to someone who writes something down. This person makes sure everyone stays on task. It's the same word used for the Egyptian officers who drove the Israelites to their hard labor in Exodus 5:6. In other words, there aren't any ants with little whips to crack on other ants if they come in late or sleep on the job or slow down the assembly line.

The third unnecessary office in the ant colony is a **ruler**. Now while ants serve the queen, who lays eggs all her life—a thousand a day or more—what Solomon means is that ants don't need a supervisor, as the word can be translated. They don't require someone to either challenge them to work or praise them when they do.[13]

As we think about these three unnecessary occupations within the ant colony, we see that:

- They don't need restrictions—that's the chief.
- They don't need requirements—that's the officer.
- And they don't need rewards—that's the ruler.

They don't need anyone to manage them, motivate them, or make them work. They are internally managed and motivated by instinct to serve for the good of the colony.

Ants Prepare for the Future

Ants seem to have an internal eye on the future. Solomon writes in verse 8 that the ant **prepares her food in the summer and gathers her provision**

in the harvest. Ants know that the season for working outside and gathering food will come to an end, and they prepare for the future.

We should consider that future day when Christ will gather us before His judgment seat and reward us for glorifying the Father through our good works (1 Corinthians 3:12-15).

- What kind of employee are you?
- What's your work ethic?
- What kind of student are you?
- How hard do you work?
- What does the teacher think when he or she sees you show up in class?
- What does your boss think of your effort and the quality of your work?

Don't forget, the review that really matters is not at the end of the fiscal year but at the feet of Christ, who will evaluate, not only the work of our hands, but also the attitude of our hearts.

No wonder Solomon writes in verse 6, **Go to the ant, O sluggard, observe her ways and be wise.** Go to the anthill; study hard and learn well. You just might be rescued from wasting your life.

Ants Serve According to Their Divinely Created Design

As we have observed, worker ants serve, the queen ant lays eggs, and soldier ants guard the mound. What are we to learn from this observation? I believe it returns us to the calling of God for every believer. Your *vocation*, your calling, happens to be your profession. Honor God in it. Consider it a sacred calling.

As a sacred calling, your vocation deserves your very best effort. A lazy Christian is a contradiction of terms. Your work is a sacred calling from the Lord designed to bring Him glory.

Ants Pool Their Strength and Resources

A final observation points to the secret of ants' endurance: Ants unite their efforts and pool their strength and resources. I have watched an ant struggling with a load, only to see another ant and then another come along and help.

What a great illustration for the family at home and the family at church. The advancement of the gospel does not normally come in big chunks of service or magnificent acts of ministry but in little acts of service.

If a church is effective in demonstrating the grace of God and delivering the gospel of Christ to people, it's only because there are people behind the scenes that we never see, uniting and pooling their strength to serve the Lord. They may never get rewarded on the platform, and they will probably go unnoticed by the majority of the church; but their faithful service in mundane matters is important to Christ and His church.

There's one occupation in particular that I think serves as a great illustration of the critical nature of our work in the gospel and our commitment to serve Christ with excellence and passion—that of a *rigger*. All branches of the military have trained riggers. Their job is to fold and pack the parachutes soldiers use when jumping from an airplane. These people are intensely dedicated to their task. The last line of the Rigger's Creed is, "I will be sure—always."[14] Riggers know jumpers need assurance that everything regarding their chutes is perfect—there is no room for error.

The Rigger's Creed further states, "I will never let the idea that a piece of work is 'good enough' make me a potential murderer through a careless mistake or oversight, for I know there can be no compromise with perfection." These dedicated riggers know that parachuting is a life-or-death enterprise. Mistakes cost lives. There is no room for complacency.

Maybe you're thinking, "That's a little too perfectionistic." Not if you jump out of an airplane with their work strapped to your back. Can you imagine being told, "Listen, your parachute was packed by that sluggard over there; we think he stayed awake and did all the folds correctly, but he's not much of a perfectionist"?

His work would matter greatly to you. *Your* work matters to God.

If God commends the ant, how much greater commendation will He have for you when you stand before Him, having served as a faithful secretary, a dedicated teacher who prepared well, a plumber who worked to get it right, a doctor who took time to listen, a cook who took pride in each meal, a salesman who cared about customers, or a student who gave every assignment your very best.

Remember, you are performing your sacred calling—your vocation—as you anticipate hearing on *that* day, "Well done, good and faithful servant."

6

THE WORD ON WORDS

Selected Proverbs

Have you ever heard something through the grapevine? If you literally placed the end of a grapevine next to your ear, you would hear *nothing*.

Travel back in time to when the abolition of slavery was gaining momentum in America, a time when runaway slaves from the south were making their way north along the Underground Railroad. The Underground Railroad was a network of safe houses that would hide, feed, and assist the fugitives to the next safe location. Cincinnati became a key location, where slaves could slip across the Ohio River on their flight to freedom.

Sympathetic people communicated with these slaves traveling the Underground Railroad through the use of laundry, strategically hung outdoors on their clothesline. One selection of clothing communicated that it was unsafe to travel in that area. Another selection of clothing identified safe houses, where food and rest could be found. Since rope was expensive in the mid-1800s, grapevines were often used as clotheslines. This primitive system of communication actually became known as the grapevine telegraph. Eventually the word *telegraph* was dropped, and people simply referred to the grapevine.[1]

Today "I heard it through the grapevine" has nothing to do with bringing people to freedom. It usually means quite the opposite.

Solomon writes to those who will join him in the quest for wisdom—the hidden treasure of insight, discernment, maturity, and grace—**Death and life are in the power of the tongue** (Proverbs 18:21). He doesn't say death and life are in the power of the *hand* but in the power of the *tongue*.

I have read that the average person has around 700 opportunities to speak every day. And the average person will speak some 12,000 sentences, using 50,000 words.

Husbands, perhaps that's why when you come home you find your wife wanting to talk. You've been talking to people all day, but she's got at least 10,000 unused sentences ready to go. And since she spent her day chasing a one-year-old around the house, none of her sentences were actually complete, so they didn't count.

Fifty thousand words a day is a book. I wonder how much of what we say would be worth writing down.

One of Solomon's favorite subjects in his collection of Proverbs is our tongue. He refers to:

- A proud tongue
- A lying tongue
- A perverse tongue
- An angry tongue
- An encouraging tongue
- A crafty tongue
- A seductive tongue
- A deceitful tongue
- A soothing tongue
- An instructive tongue
- A flattering tongue
- A guarded tongue
- A quiet tongue
- A crass tongue

And on and on the list goes.

God has a lot to say about what *we* say!

Let's tackle this expansive topic by dividing our observations into two sections: how our words can help others, and how our words can hurt others.

HOW WORDS CAN HELP

Words Can Provide Good Counsel.

Proverbs 27:9 says, **Oil and perfume make the heart glad, so a man's counsel is sweet to his friend.** The influence of a friend's counsel is unparalleled. That's why we must be very careful about whom we allow to counsel us.

One of God's intended benefits for a body of believers is that we together admonish one another. Paul writes:

> Let the word of Christ richly dwell within you, with all wisdom teaching and admonishing one another with psalms and hymns and spiritual songs, singing with thankfulness in your hearts to God. (Colossians 3:16)

The Greek word usually translated "admonish" is *noutheteō*. It means to "put one in mind" of the truth. Biblical counseling is sometimes referred to as *nouthetic* counseling. It is essentially biblical admonition.

We should be asking then, "Did that conversation I just had with another believer counsel them or corrupt them?" Our daily conversations are actually mutual counseling sessions whereby we exchange the reassurance and advice that help us deal with the routine challenges of life.[2]

Words Can Confront

With confrontation comes the idea of correction. The words we use offer not only advice but also accountability.

Solomon writes in Proverbs 17:10, **A rebuke goes deeper into one who has understanding than a hundred blows into a fool.** If we confront committed believers about things they are doing or saying that miss the mark of holy living, they will consider our words—deeply.

We use the expression, "A word to the wise is sufficient." Just a word or two, and a wise person will listen and learn from his mistakes, accept the word of admonition, yield to authority, and take appropriate action. Not so a fool, Solomon writes here in chapter 17. Even if he's beaten black and blue with a hundred strokes of a rod, he will go back to his folly.[3]

Solomon also warns, **Do not reprove a scoffer, or he will hate you, reprove a wise man and he will love you** (Proverbs 9:8). Not everyone you confront or challenge will love you in return.

Correction may take the courage of Nathan, who confronted David over murder and adultery with Bathsheba. It might take the boldness of Joab, who confronted David, telling him his unbounded grieving over Absalom was hurting his integrity as a ruler.[4] To his credit, David listened in both instances (2 Samuel 12, 15).

Words Can Comfort

In Proverbs 25:11, the Bible says, **Like apples of gold in settings of silver is a word spoken in right circumstances.**

Charles Bridges wrote in the mid-1800s that this is literal fruit—golden apples—served on silver trays.[5] How refreshing, then, are words—like ripe fruit—that come served in the finest way possible, satisfying both hunger and thirst at the same time.

Words Can Cheer

Solomon writes, **A soothing tongue is a tree of life, but perversion in it crushes the spirit** (Proverbs 15:4). Words have the power of life-changing encouragement.

Listen to sports announcers talking about "home field advantage." Playing in front of people who are screaming encouraging things rather than things you can't repeat is certainly an advantage. When fans are friends instead of foes, a team will likely play at their best.

Has it ever occurred to you that the believer's battles are all "away games"? We are far from home. The world is cheering for the opposing side and hoping for our defeat and despair. The noise in the stadiums of our world system is sometimes overpowering.

The only time we'll hear words of encouragement is when we're in the huddle with our teammates. The assembly, the church, is our huddle. So, let's cheer one another on. The writer of Hebrews says to encourage one another "as you see the day drawing near" (Hebrews 10:25). What day? The day of Christ's coming. The day when the contest is over.

One author wrote about entering a half-ironman triathlon. He was a pastor who just wanted to have this accomplishment in the bag. He wrote:

> After the 1.2 mile swim and the 56-mile bike ride, I didn't have much energy left for the 13.1 mile run. Neither did the fellow jogging next to me. I asked him how he was doing and soon regretted posing the question. "This stinks. This race is the dumbest decision I've ever made." He had more complaints than a taxpayer at the IRS. My response to him? "Good-bye." I knew if I listened too long, I'd start agreeing with him.
>
> I caught up with a sixty-six-year-old grandmother. Her tone was just the opposite. "You'll finish this," she encouraged. "It's hot, but at least it's not raining. One step at a time. . . . Don't forget to hydrate. . . . Stay in there." I ran next to her until my heart was lifted and my legs were aching. I finally had to slow down. "No problem," she said, waving as she kept going.[6]

Which runner represents you and your words as you jog alongside others in the race of faith?

Words Can Be Constructive

Paul wrote to the Thessalonians, "Build up one another, just as you also are doing" (1 Thessalonians 5:11). He wrote further, "We urge you, brethren . . . encourage the fainthearted, help the weak" (verse 14).

Solomon puts it this way: **The lips of the righteous feed many** (Proverbs 10:21). And in Proverbs 15:7 he writes, **The lips of the wise spread knowledge**.

This is the edifying, strengthening effect of words. Christians should speak words that are constructive, wisely counseling, confronting, comforting, and cheering one another along.

HOW WORDS CAN HURT

Words Can Deceive

Proverbs 6:17 lists **a lying tongue** among seven things that God hates. Satan's first recorded words in human history were all lies. "Eat this and you will be as wise as God," he promised Eve (see Genesis 3:1-5).

Solomon has a short prayer list, and at the head of it is this: **Keep deception and lies far from me** (Proverbs 30:8). What he's really praying is to be kept from the influence of, and the imitation of, the great Deceiver.[7] He recognizes, as we all should, that we have the devilish ability to imitate our former father, Satan, who is the father of lies (John 8:44).

Words Can Destroy

Remember the child's chant, "Sticks and stones may break my bones, but words will never hurt me"? That's a lie too, isn't it? In reality, sticks and stones are easy to endure compared to words.

I don't carry any scars from sticks or stones, except for a little scar at the corner of my right eye. When I was around six or seven years old, I was out in the front yard throwing a large rock up in the air and catching it. Eventually I missed.

Rocks can hurt, but words hang on. Words have the ability to tear down everything from friendships to marriages to churches.

Solomon writes in Proverbs 18:6, **A fool's lips bring strife, and his mouth calls for blows**. A fool eventually starts a fight. His words ignite controversy and division in which everybody loses. Let him keep talking, and somebody's reputation will be ruined; somebody's name will be dirtied; somebody's spirit will be crushed.

In seminary one of our pastoral theology professors warned us about the destructive power of gossip. He told us about a pastor and his wife who were barely meeting their bills, serving Christ faithfully in their small church. There was a successful businessman in the church who was an immense help to the pastor and his family.

On one occasion the pastor was invited to preach in a meeting in another city several hours away. He didn't have money for a plane ticket, and his own car was too old to risk the drive. When this businessman found out about it, he told the pastor that he had to fly out of town during this same time period. It was the perfect solution. He told the pastor, "Listen, why don't you drive over to my home, drop off your car, take me to the airport and then take off for your meeting in my new car. Then you can pick me up when we both get back into town."

The only problem with this perfect plan was that the pastor now had his vehicle parked overnight at this man's home, while the businessman's car was gone. The neighbors jumped to conclusions—and spread the word. In a matter of days that little community had heard the gossip.

The pastor ended up resigning, unable to overcome the destruction to his reputation and integrity. There was no way he could compete with the grapevine that had spread the gossip like cancer all over that little town. Solomon writes, **With his mouth, the godless man destroys his neighbor** (Proverbs 11:9).

Words Can Divide

Proverbs 16:28 says, **A slanderer separates intimate friends**. This person is more than happy to hang dirty laundry out in the open whenever possible. What is startling about Solomon's statement isn't that *acquaintances* are separated—church members who hardly know each other—but that close *friends* are divided.

This was such a serious problem in the early church that nearly every New Testament epistle deals with the danger. Paul bluntly tells Titus to dismiss the divisive person from the assembly after a second warning. This isn't traditional church discipline where witnesses are brought to bear and the congregation is brought into the process to woo and warn the wayward brother. No, Paul says, "Reject a factious [divisive] man after a first and second warning" (Titus 3:10).

Why? Because the church is to demonstrate unity in the Spirit and the transforming power of the gospel to produce love and good works; and the enemy will use a divisive person's words to handicap the church's ability to demonstrate that unity.

So, the question remains: What are *we* to do about this dangerous power we carry around in our mouths?"

WHAT WE SHOULD DO

Secure Our Words

Solomon writes, **He who guards his mouth and his tongue, guards his soul from troubles** (Proverbs 21:23). Isn't that the truth! We should have learned this in third grade. I was never sent to the corner of the room for being *quiet.*

Before we began homeschooling our sons, they attended a public elementary school. When they were in second grade, we were sitting at the dinner table, and one of my sons said, "Hey, Dad, I think our music teacher is a Christian." His brother chimed in, "Yeah, we're pretty sure he's a Christian." I thought, *Man, my sons are really discerning about spiritual things at such a young age.* I asked them, "Well, how do you know?" They said, "Well, we were all misbehaving in class, and he went over to the corner . . . we could tell he was praying."

He probably was. And here's what he might have been praying, "Set a guard, O Lord, over my mouth; keep watch over the door of my lips" (Psalm 141:3).

What a great prayer: "Lord, post guards at the door of my lips. Don't let anything out without clearance from You."

Silence Our Words

Solomon records, **He who restrains his lips is wise** (Proverbs 10:19). Abraham Lincoln once wrote, "I have often regretted my speech, never my silence."

Let me recommend that you *burn* the grapevine. Treat it like that poison ivy vine you have out by the back fence that keeps trying to come back. Stay away from internet friends if you're having trouble staying out of the gossip mill.

Solomon writes, **He who restrains his words has knowledge** (Proverbs 17:27). In other words, one of the smartest things we can do sometimes is bite our tongue.

Sweeten Our Words

"Keep your words sweet," someone once said; "you never know when you might have to eat them." Solomon puts it this way in Proverbs 16:24: **Pleasant words are a honeycomb.**

Ray Pritchard writes that it takes eight to ten positive comments to offset one negative comment. In other words, eight to ten loving, caring, kind words are needed to erase the effects of one hurtful, unkind, unloving, careless word that was written on the blackboard of someone's mind.[8]

What are some pleasant words worth repeating?

I'm Proud of You

These words are sweet to the soul. Letting some special people know you've noticed them, you admire them, and you're acknowledging their contributions is wind in their sails.

Perhaps it's been too long, dad, for your child to hear those words. Perhaps it's been too long, young man or young woman, for your parents to hear those words from you.

I Forgive You

With the exception of "I love you," these are perhaps the most powerful words in the English language. They are life-giving, hope-filled, reconciling words.

A man came up to me some time ago and said, "I took your advice and contacted my estranged wife, and I just admitted I had been wrong and asked her to forgive me." And with tears streaming down his cheeks, unable to hardly get the next sentence out, he said, "And my wife said, 'I forgive you.'"

A relationship between a son and a father, a businessman and a client, two believers caught in conflict, a teacher and a student, or an employee and a boss can be turned from darkness and despair to light and hope with the humility and grace offered in these three simple words: I forgive you.

Thank You

Say this to your waitress, your dentist, and the nursery worker when you pick up your child after church. Sweet words require humility. To thank someone is to admit that you benefited from that person's assistance. Humble words are helpful words.

Husbands, how long has it been since you said "Thank you" to your wife for the myriad of things she does for you? When's the last time you thanked your wife for supper? "Thank you, honey; that was delicious." If you can't say it was delicious, then, "Thank you, honey; that was . . . unforgettable."

Let's be wise with our words, realizing that with them we can counsel, confront, comfort, cheer, and be constructive. But let's also be warned that with our words we can deceive, destroy, and divide.

Here's a closing prayer worth repeating:

> Lord, fill my mouth with worthwhile stuff,
> And nudge me when I've said enough.

Enough said.

7

THE ULTIMATE FATHER-SON CHAT

Proverbs 4:1-9

Several years ago, I came across the unusual story of Larry Walters. I even saw a picture of his famous lawn chair.

It seems that Larry had a lifelong dream to fly. When he graduated from high school, he joined the Air Force in hopes of becoming a pilot. Unfortunately, his poor eyesight ended that particular dream.

When he left the service, he enjoyed sitting out in his lawn chair, watching the jets that crisscrossed the skies over his backyard. Then one day, Larry Walters got an idea. With the help of his girlfriend, he bought some helium tanks and weather balloons from the local Army-Navy surplus store.

They filled the balloons, which had been tied to his lawn chair, which in turn was anchored by a rope to the bumper of his jeep. He climbed into the lawn chair with some sandwiches and drinks and his trusty BB gun. His plan was to hover in the air at a comfortable height and then pop a few of the balloons when it was time to settle back down to earth.

Lawn-chair Larry, as he was about to become known around the world, cut the rope on July 2, 1982. But he didn't float gently up; he shot upward as if fired from a cannon, and he didn't stop ascending until he leveled off at 16,000 feet—three miles above the earth. Too terrified to shoot any of the balloons, which might cause an imbalance and toss him out of his lawn chair, he simply hung on for dear life.

He eventually drifted from San Pedro, California into the approach corridor for the Los Angeles International Airport. A pilot radioed the tower about "passing a guy in a lawn chair."

A rescue helicopter was dispatched, but every time it got near him, the current of wind pushed him dangerously away. Finally, Larry got up the nerve and shot one balloon and then another and another, and he slowly descended, until the balloons got caught in a power line, causing a neighborhood in Long Beach to experience a blackout! He was, however, able to climb down, whereupon he was immediately arrested.

Imagine that final indignity, being put under arrest by law enforcement who were scratching their heads to try to figure out what to charge him with. They ended up charging him with "operating an aircraft without an airworthiness certificate," and "not maintaining contact with air traffic control."

As he was being led away by LAPD, a reporter asked him why he did it, and Larry responded, "A man can't just sit around."[1]

Obviously, he should have sat around a little longer—and thought it through more clearly! Maybe he could have experimented first—you know, with two balloons and the neighbor's cat.

When I read this story again recently, I wondered if he'd thought through some details:

- What about low-flying aircraft?
- What if the balloons burst or leaked?
- Were the ropes strong enough and tied well enough to keep the balloons and the chair connected?
- How do you steer a lawn chair?

I couldn't help but think that parenting is a lot like Larry's flight. There's no time to experiment. The couple arrive at the hospital in time, and before the new parents are ready or hardly prepared, they're moved out. "Hey, insurance only covers forty-eight hours . . . we need this room."

Just to show you how things have changed, when Marsha delivered our twins at Baylor Hospital in Dallas back in the 1980s, she was in the hospital for four days—the standard length of time. And before we checked out, we were served a full-course dinner in their special parlor for new parents. It was standard operating procedure for all new parents at the hospital—steak and baked potato cooked to order.

I don't think hospitals do that anymore.

When you finally arrive home, you have a baby bed, a dresser filled with little outfits, and plenty of pajamas with footies. There are cases of baby lotion and baby powder and a plastic tub for bath time and on and on and on. Most of it's on loan or borrowed from friends, except for the car seat—that was a special purchase that required a second mortgage. It morphs from a car seat into a stroller into a high chair.

Before you know it, you're airborne—traveling higher and faster and farther away from everything you know or ever planned. You can't catch your breath, and days are sometimes exhilarating but most of the time exhausting.

Well-meaning friends drop in to help or give advice or give you the latest book on the personality development of eight-week-olds and how you can really mess them up if you get it wrong.

You soon discover there may be a formula you can feed a child, but there's no formula to raising one. Each child is unique and different. And by the time you figure out the basics of parenting, the ride is over and you're under arrest—I mean, you're an empty nester.

For young parents and old and even for grandparents who are flying in *that* new territory for the first time, God actually has a lot to say about what really matters. Proverbs, in particular, has important instruction for parents. It won't be about what kind of diaper increases children's IQ, or where they're supposed to be on the percentage scale of three-week-olds, or why they must be able to crawl by six months and walk by ten if they are to be superior human beings. By the way, one of our sons never learned how to crawl properly. He just pulled himself along with one arm, like some wounded soldier crawling under a fence. I was convinced at the time that this child—who would later be named to the all-state soccer team—evidently wasn't able to do stuff babies are supposed to do.

According to what God reveals in His Word, He doesn't seem worried about percentage points or diaper selection.

Ask the average father today if he's had "the talk" with his middle schooler or high schooler, and he will respond, "You mean *the* talk?" "Oh yeah. Have you had the talk?" Ask him what "the talk" is about, and he'll say it has something to do with the birds and bees, right?

Now, it's not wrong to have that talk. In fact, Solomon spends quite a bit of time talking about the dangers of being sexually involved with someone you're not married to.

But what I find fascinating is that while most fathers who agree that they must have a talk with their sons or daughters about sexual matters will rarely talk about the character of God, eternal life, election, eternal security, grace, giving, and so on. What children truly need is for parents to communicate biblical truth about character and virtues and priorities and integrity and submission to God.

Frankly, God knew we would need direction concerning *what* to talk about with our children, and He has given us plenty of guidance on the subject matter. In fact, Proverbs chapter 4 presents what I call the ultimate father-son chat. We find here two principles of wise parental counsel.

THE PRINCIPLE OF SPIRITUAL EDIFICATION

The objective of this principle is telling children the truth. Solomon writes in Proverbs 4:1: **Hear, O sons, the instruction of a father.**

This is the first and only time in this chapter where the plural "sons" appears. Since the chapter switches later to the singular, it seems that Solomon is making sure his words are understood as good advice for *all* sons—in fact for *all* children.

Another thing to keep in mind is that although the father is mentioned in this text, both parents are responsible for the teaching process. Solomon writes in chapter 1 verse 8, "Hear, my son, your father's instruction and do not forsake your mother's teaching." Likewise, in chapter 6 he writes, "My son, observe the commandment of your father and do not forsake the teaching of your mother" (verse 20).

It's clear that the teaching of both mother and father are instructive and necessary in the development of the child. However, it seems that here in chapter 4 the Spirit of God is focusing the lens of inspired Scripture on the father.

Fathers play a significant role in communicating to their children the truth about what God has said. They must teach them *who* God is and *what*

He expects. They must build them up in the faith—this is the principle and priority of edification.

This was Paul's desire toward his children in the faith when he reminded them that "speaking the truth in love, we are to grow up in all aspects into Him who is the head, even Christ . . . [causing] the growth of the body for the building up [edification] of itself in love" (Ephesians 4:15-16).

Solomon's father-son chat is based on delivering the truth in love. He writes in Proverbs 4:2, **For I give you sound teaching; do not abandon my instruction**.

But isn't this text a command to the *child* to listen to the father deliver the truth? Yes, but it also implies that the father has something worth hearing.

The word **instruction** in verse 2 is the translation of the Hebrew word *torah*, or "law." It's the law and the statutes and the principles of God's Word. This is what fathers are to teach their sons. This text is revealing a very personal father-son encounter relating to the teaching of the truth of God.[2]

This principle of spiritual edification is expanded in Deuteronomy 6:7, where Moses writes:

> "You shall teach them [God's commands] diligently to your sons and shall talk of them when you sit in your house and when you walk by the way and when you lie down and when you rise up."

What a wonderful text. We build up and strengthen our children when we make the Word of God our common theme. This is not an event on our calendar that starts at 7:00 a.m. or ends with a bedtime story. This is a *lifestyle*—talking about God's Word while sitting, walking, lying down, and getting up in the morning.

Your children have questions about spiritual things that you can't always schedule and you might not even be prepared to answer.

Someone compiled a list of questions elementary school kids had written to God:

- "Dear God," Neil wrote, "I went to this wedding, and they kissed right in church. Is that OK?"

- "Dear God," another wrote, "in Bible times, did they really talk that fancy?"
- Robert prayed, "Dear God, I am an American. What are You?"
- "Dear God," Jane asked, "instead of letting people die and having to make new ones, why don't You just keep the ones you got now?"

Some of them didn't have questions, but they had something they wanted to say.

- Jonathan wrote, "Dear God, if You didn't let the dinosaurs go extinct, we would not have a country. You did the right thing."
- Nan wrote, "I bet it is very hard for You to love everybody in the whole world. There are four people in my family, and I can't do it."
- Joyce must have felt the same way when she wrote, "Dear God, thank You for my baby brother, but what I prayed for was a puppy."
- Elliot wrote, "Dear God, I think about You sometimes even when I'm not praying."[3]

I wondered as I read Elliot's prayer if his parents have any idea that there are times when Elliot thinks about God. Who's going to answer his questions and guide his thoughts?

Why is it that most moms do the bedtime reading? That's a great place for dads to get involved. You never know what you'll hear. In those unguarded moments, spiritual truths can be reiterated with simple yet profound meaning.

THE PRINCIPLE OF SPIRITUAL IMITATION

The first principle, spiritual edification, requires mentoring. This second principle, spiritual imitation, requires modeling.

Mom and dad, it's one thing to lecture about the truth; it's another thing to live out the truth. Even in moments when we fail, we have an opportunity to model genuine confession as we ask the Lord—and perhaps our children—for forgiveness.

Isn't it great for our kids to know that we know how to confess our sins? We can teach them by example that our Lord is indeed "faithful and righteous to forgive us our sins and to cleanse us from all unrighteousness" (1 John 1:9).

Solomon writes in Proverbs 4:3: **When I was a son to my father**. This is not so much a reference to biological kinship as it is submission to the father's counsel.[4]

Don't miss this. Solomon is saying to his son—more than likely a reference specifically to Rehoboam—"Let me tell you what Grandpa said." Then he continues in verse 4: **He [that is, your grandfather David] taught me and said to me, "Let your heart hold fast my words; keep my commandments and live."**

Solomon is accomplishing a couple of things here. First, he's *reinforcing his advice with the past.* He says, "Listen, Rehoboam, when I was a son like you, I heard the same thing."

This sounds a lot like, "Let me tell you about when I was a boy. I used to walk three miles to a one-room schoolhouse in the snow. So, stop complaining about your bus ride at 6:30 in the morning.

"And be grateful for the lunch you have; don't waste it. Why, when I was a boy, the lunch I took to that one-room schoolhouse was a raw potato. That's what most of the farm boys brought. And we'd each put our potato on top of that black, wood-burning stove during school, and by lunchtime it would be cooked through and ready to eat. I'd have a little wrapped pat of butter in my pocket, and that potato and butter would be my lunch."

You might say, "Oh, come on. Nobody did that." My father actually did. He walked to a one-room schoolhouse out in the farmland of Minnesota, carrying his potato and butter for lunch.

How do you complain about not having butterscotch pudding in your lunch box after a story like that? And that's not to mention the stories of my grandfather arriving in Minnesota in a covered wagon.

There is something powerful about a heritage that passes on to us the contexts of gratitude and grace and courage and grit and determination and honest work and speaking the truth. Tell your children stories about *your* childhood. Trust me, they will think yours are just as strange. Let them know how you might have struggled or felt out of place. Tell them how the Word of God intersected your life.

Tell your children how and when you accepted Christ. That's way more important than the "birds and the bees," learning to drive a car, opening a bank account, or dressing for success. The truth of God and about God and for the pleasure of God is the subject of the ultimate father-son chat.

Solomon is essentially saying here, "When I was a boy, I received this instruction from your grandfather David. He wasn't perfect, but he tried to model obedience to God's instruction. Now I'm giving this hidden treasure to you. God's Word mattered back then, and it matters today, and it will matter into your future."

Second, Solomon not only reinforces his advice with the past, but he also *identifies with his son in the present*. He says in verse 3, **When I was a son to my father, tender and the only son in the sight of my mother**. That word **tender** can be translated "pliable" or "weak" and conveys the idea of being impressionable.

Solomon is basically saying, "I know what it's like to be young. I know how you feel. Just as your grandfather told me when I was young, I'm now passing along to you this fatherly advice." And what is that advice? **Acquire wisdom! Acquire understanding! Do not forget nor turn away from the words of my mouth. . . . she [wisdom] will guard you . . . she will watch over you** (verses 5-6).

Get wisdom!

How many fathers say, "Get a haircut . . . get your room cleaned . . . get a job . . . get an education"? But how many say, "Whatever you do, get wisdom . . . nothing matters more than finding the hidden treasure of wisdom!"

You can be an educated fool. You can be highly paid and miserable. You can be the best dressed and the most likely to succeed but destroy every relationship through pride.

Get wisdom—first and foremost.

This is the urgency of a father toward his son. Solomon writes further in verses 8-9:

> **Prize her [wisdom], and she will exalt you; she will honor you if you embrace her. She will place on your head a garland of grace; she will present you with a crown of beauty.**

"Son, let me tell you what will make you stand up and stand out, what will draw people to you. It has nothing to do with how you look, or what you own, or what you wear; it has to do with who you are and whom you serve. Prize and pursue wisdom."

Wisdom delivers lasting grace and beauty. These are not physical attributes in this context; they are the fruit of wisdom in the inner attitude and spirit.

You want to have a father-son (or parent-child) chat? For starters, it's not a one-time event. It's an ongoing conversation that takes place as life happens. It's a mentoring and modeling process. It's recognizing that you will always be a parent and you will always be somebody's child.

How blessed are children whose parents care deeply about the hidden treasure of wisdom and communicate it to the next generation by means of edification and imitation.

Charlie Shedd not only taught and modeled godly wisdom to his children, but he also wrote much of it down for them to have later in life. Some of his letters to his children were eventually published as books.

In a letter to his son Peter, he told of a trip to the country he had with Peter's older brother Philip.

> We had been out in the country for a ride. It was evening and we ran out of gas. We were walking along after we had been to the farm house, and I was carrying a can of gas. Philip was only four. He was playing along, throwing rocks at the telephone poles, picking flowers, and then, all of a sudden it got dark. Sometimes night comes all at once in the country. Philip came over, put his little hand in mine and said, "Take my hand, Daddy. I might get lost."

Charlie then added, "Peter, there is a hand reaching to you from the heart of the universe. If you will lay your hand in the hand of God and walk with Him, you will never ever get lost."[5] What a wonderful truth and what lasting encouragement.

This is the truth that our children and grandchildren must hear from our lips. This is the truth they must see modeled in our lives.

Now, it might not change your child's life. We can't know for sure. But it will change *yours*.

And that's the best place to begin.

8

FINDING WISDOM IN THE WOODSHED

Selected Proverbs

If you study through the book of Proverbs, sooner or later you're going to be confronted with the subject of parental authority and, more specifically, the disciplining of children. Talk about a controversial subject!

NECESSITY OF BIBLICAL DISCIPLINE

There are numerous proverbs in Solomon's collection that most people you live around or work with today would consider out of date and out of touch. Here's one, for example: **He who withholds his rod hates his son, but he who loves him disciplines him diligently** (Proverbs 13:24). Here's another, Proverbs 22:15: **Foolishness is bound up in the heart of a child; the rod of discipline will remove it far from him.** Most people today would say, "No wonder that stuff is in the Old Testament. That's where it belongs—in ancient history."

But consider this proverb: **The rod and reproof give wisdom, but a child who gets his own way brings shame to his mother** (Proverbs 29:15). Whether conservative or liberal, churched or unchurched, converted to Christ or an atheist, everyone knows that a child who gets his way is going to bring shame on his mother and father. You've never heard any parent brag, "Our son refused our help and all our advice. He's since left home and lives at the Rescue Mission and panhandles in the parking lot of the mall. We're so thrilled with what he's doing with his life."

All parents, whether they think the Word of God should be relegated to ancient history or not, know intuitively that their child is better off when he or she walks wisely.

According to Proverbs 29:15, **The rod and reproof give wisdom**. That truth might come as a surprise to you.

We are not only to hunt for the hidden treasures of wisdom ourselves, but as parents we are to help our children discover those treasures as well. And Solomon says here that the rod literally serves as part of the treasure map. Imagine that—wisdom is found in the woodshed.

Now, we'll balance this out as we make several observations, but you ought to know that the Hebrew word for **rod** [*shebet*] can be translated "club."

My mom didn't know that; she thought it meant a "switch." She would send me out to the tree that was just outside the kitchen screen door to select the switch that would be used to communicate wisdom and drive folly from my heart. I'm just glad she didn't know any Hebrew. She would have taken this literally, being the good dispensationalist that she is. One thing is for certain, though: she *believed* this verse.

Today, most parents will do anything but spank their child. They might say that spanking children will teach them to hit other children. Trust me, our children know how to hit other children whether we spank them or not. In fact, with all the spankings *I* received, it never crossed my mind to do to some schoolmate what my parents did to me.

Some parents refuse to admit their child *needs* correction. They will argue his innocence with the teacher, the principle, the youth leader, and, later on, the policeman. Perhaps it's nothing more than pride, unwilling to face the humiliation of a child in need of correction. Naturally, we all want our children to be at the head of the class, *not* sent to the corner of the class or expelled from class.

Maybe you've struggled with these proverbs because you came from a home where discipline was nothing more than physical abuse, where hate and anger spilled over and spankings became beatings. There is a vast difference between what you experienced and what the Bible teaches.

I have a few books I want to recommend to every parent with a son or daughter still living at home. One is *Shepherding a Child's Heart*, by Tedd Tripp.[1] For moms who want to read additional material, Ginger Plowman has given similar counsel geared toward younger children. Her book is entitled, *Don't Make Me Count to Three.*[2] Perhaps you can identify with making that threat.

While I'm at it, another excellent work is called *Family Life*, by Chuck Swindoll, and it covers a variety of issues. My copy at home is dog-eared and has been marked up over the years.[3] In Swindoll's work, he quotes Dr. Albert Siegel who wrote this in the *Stanford Observer*:

> When it comes to rearing children, every society is only twenty years away from barbarism. Twenty years is all we have to accomplish the task of civilizing the infants who are born into our midst each year. These savages know nothing of our language, our culture, our religion, our values, customs of interpersonal relations. The infant is totally ignorant about . . . respect, decency, honesty, customs, manners and conventions. The barbarian must be tamed if civilization is to survive.[4]

This powerfully expresses the need for discipline. Still, this falls short of true and full reformation since we *can* have educated, self-controlled people destroying society just as easily as barbarians.

Biblical discipline deals not only with behavior but also with attitude and heart and spirit. We understand the greater issue is the corruption of the heart; sinful, fallen creatures need redemption and spiritual growth, not just superficial changes. That's why Solomon writes in Proverbs 29:15 that it isn't just the rod but reproof, verbal correction, that reaches for the heart.

The Lord said in Luke 6:45:

> "The good man out of the good treasure of his heart brings forth what is good; and the evil man out of the evil treasure brings forth what is evil; for his mouth speaks from that which fills his heart."

That reminds every parent of *the heart* of the matter. A child's misbehavior reflects that child's spirit. We can get so sidetracked with behavior that we overlook the real issue of the heart and what our children believe. It's easy to think that if we can just correct our children's behavior, we've succeeded. But they can still believe that lying is acceptable, that obedience is optional, that cheating is permissible.[5]

That was the point of Christ's warning to the Pharisees, who kept all the rules and never missed synagogue services. They lived moral lives and spoke respectfully of God with their lips, which had nothing to do with their hearts (Matthew 15). A change in behavior that does not stem from a change in heart is not commended by Christ; it is hypocrisy of the highest order.[6]

Whether we want to admit it or not, Solomon was telling the truth when he wrote in Proverbs 22:15, **Foolishness is bound up in the heart of a child**. In other words, children are born with the ability to lie, cheat, disobey, and declare their own will. And very early in life they make it clear *they* want to be in charge.

About a century ago the Minnesota Crime Commission released an interesting report on the untamed child. I can't imagine this kind of report being released in the twenty-first century, but look at these words from this 1926 document:

> Every baby starts life as a little savage. He is completely selfish and self-centered. He wants what he wants when he wants it; his bottle, his mother's attention, his playmate's toys, his uncle's watch, or whatever. Deny him these and he seethes with rage and aggressiveness which would be murderous were he not so helpless. . . . This means that all children, not just certain children but all children, are born delinquent. If permitted to continue in their self-centered world of infancy, given free rein to their impulsive actions to satisfy each want, every child would grow up a criminal.[7]

Frankly put, mom and dad, you're dealing with a little sinner, who came into the world with a fallen, depraved heart. And that child is capable of committing anything under the sun, given the time, experience, availability, resources, and strength. When Solomon wrote, **Foolishness is bound up in the heart of a child**, the Hebrew word he used for **foolishness** refers to moral corruption and the inability to reason and make good judgments.

That's why you never had to teach your children how to lie; you had to discipline them to be honest. You never had to teach them to be selfish; you had to instruct them to share. You never had to teach them to assert themselves; you had to teach them to submit to authority.

Long before they learn to talk, they challenge your authority. Just tell that seven-month-old, "Honey, don't touch that," and what does little honey do? She looks you square in the face, never blinking an eye, and reaches her hand out to touch it again. She's effectively saying, "I am in charge around here. . . didn't you get the memo?"

Solomon gives parents hope. The end of that proverb reads, **Discipline will remove it far from him** (Proverbs 22:15).

That won't happen quickly. It requires a commitment to consistent, daily discipline, in imitation of God, who consistently disciplines all His children (Hebrews 12:5-6) and is still working to drive from us rebellion and pride.

In disciplining our children, we are actually initiating a godly process that *God* will take over one day in their lives. And if we have taught them to listen to us, they will be prepared to listen to Him.

Given the heart of a child—which is a sinful, rebellious *human* heart—discipline is a necessary part of parenting. The Bible, and Proverbs in particular, makes this very clear.

DISCERNMENT IN BIBLICAL DISCIPLINE

It's important to remember that biblical discipline is not solely about physical discipline, or what we often call corporal punishment. Again, Proverbs 29:15 says, **The rod *and* reproof give wisdom**. The two go hand in hand. Physical discipline, the **rod**, must always be accompanied by verbal communication in the form of **reproof** that corrects and instructs. The rod of discipline, however, is a major emphasis in Proverbs, and in light of the present-day rejection of it, we especially need to address it.

The use of the rod—call it simply spanking—must not be an immediate, thoughtless, angry response to every failure on the part of our children. Discernment is needed to avoid overreaction and inappropriate use of spanking.

We Need to Distinguish Between Physical Abuse and a Painful Spanking

People today are quick to label the biblical discipline of spanking as physical abuse. There is a world of difference between the two, as the helpful chart below reflects. As Christians, we need to know and observe these distinctions. There is no place in a Christian home for physical abuse.

Abuse[8]	**Discipline**
Unprovoked and unexpected	Expected for certain behavior (it's already been made clear; there are no surprises)
Motivated by hatred and anger	Prompted by love and concern
Produces terror	Produces security
Leaves physical scars	Painful but doesn't leave scars
Creates resentment against authority	Creates respect for authority
Resolves neither behavior nor heart attitude	Resolves, forgives, and forgets

We must clearly distinguish between abuse and discipline, both in word and practice.

We Must Distinguish Between Immaturity and Disobedience

Deliberate disobedience needs to be dealt with, but we must understand that young children simply lack maturity. They may, in fact, forget, or get sidetracked with the dog, or completely overlook what time it is. In many cases, patient instruction, not spanking, may be more appropriate.

We Must Distinguish Between Inability and Defiance

Maybe they really can't fulfill that task we assigned to them. For them, cleaning out the shed might be something that overwhelms them, and they're not sure where to start or how to do it. Again, we should not punish them for defiance when it's really a matter of inability.

PRACTICE OF BIBLICAL DISCIPLINE

Now, what if it's clear you're dealing with an act of disobedience, or disrespect, or deception? Well, those are the three D's that I believe require a trip to the woodshed—disobedience, disrespect, and deception. Let me give you five guidelines for finding wisdom in the woodshed.

Explain What the Offense Is and What the Punishment Will Be

This eliminates the possibility of spanking the child in the heat of the moment or in anger. It allows for communication before the punishment, which helps the child to understand the issue at hand is not his parent's emotions but his own sinful actions.

Deliver the Spanking

It might be three swats or ten licks on the place God created for discipline—in fact, He created it with extra padding. Slapping or punching a child is demeaning and inappropriate. Further, it isn't using the rod, and it will never yield the intimacy and closeness that comes after proper discipline is administered.

The rod, not your hand, creates the pain; and in the mystery of discipline, your children come to fear the leather strap or the switch or the paddle. They do not come to fear your hand.

Give the Child Time to Think and Recover

Depending on your child's age, you might leave the room, and give her time to dry her tears. The younger children are, the more immediately they need the reassurance of your love.

I remember whenever one of our daughters received a spanking when she was a little girl—and it was often—she would immediately raise her arms for me to pick her up and tell her she was loved and forgiven. As children get older, you might leave the room for a brief period of time and then return to talk to them.

Explain What God's Word Says about the Child's Sinful Behavior and Attitude

In a very personal conversation, deal with your child's heart issue. In fact, after punishment he or she is more open and ready to hear about underlying heart issues. Biblical discipline is not just about delivering a painful spanking for disobedience; the pain in discipline acts as the doorway through which the heart is now tender and open to receive true wisdom.

It's appropriate to read or quote a Bible passage that deals with what the enemy wanted to accomplish through their sin. It's the perfect time to explain that the issue is larger than a lie or a stolen object or disrespect. It may very well be a lifelong—or eternal—issue.

Solomon wrote, **You shall strike him with the rod and rescue his soul from Sheol [or death]** (Proverbs 23:14). This is a general principle that means discipline normally protects your child from greater harm. That's why you might spank your children when they disobey you by running into the street. You want to associate pain with their disobedience, which very well may save them *greater* pain, perhaps even death.

You are also teaching them, especially older children, what one author called the "harvest mentality." That is, they are learning the principle that they will reap what they sow.

So, lead them to pray, asking the Lord for forgiveness, because ultimately, they need to recognize that they have sinned against the Lord, not just mom or dad.

After Prayer, Hug the Child and Speak Words that Clearly Communicate, "I Love You, and I Have Forgiven You"

This is the perfect resolution to biblical discipline. I remember getting a spanking from my father and fifteen minutes later laughing and playing basketball with him in the backyard.

It was never a question of love for me. I never thought he didn't love me. I just knew he loved Christ first. And I knew he was obeying the Word of God, which deepened my respect for him. I knew in disciplining me, both my parents were ultimately demonstrating love for Christ and love for me.

This is exactly what Solomon meant when he wrote: **He who withholds his rod *hates* his son, but he who *loves* him disciplines him diligently** (Proverbs 13:24).

TRUTHS OF BIBLICAL DISCIPLINE

Let me offer two timeless truths about the subject of biblical, parental discipline.

There Has Never Been an Easy Time to Raise Children

Ask Adam and Eve. Ask Eli and, later, Samuel. Ask David and Solomon. Just ask Mary and Joseph, whose entire brood of children, born after Jesus, stubbornly refused to believe Him until *after* His resurrection.

No generation has been without unique dangers and temptations. There's never been a perfect century to be a parent—we live in a fallen world.

Yes, these are particularly challenging times as we watch the American culture fall into the final stages of disintegration and disarray. One author observes some common characteristics that *every* decaying culture experiences:

- An increased ability to divorce easily and without cause
- The elimination of meaning in the marriage ceremony
- Pessimism concerning earlier cultural figures who had been revered/considered heroic
- The breaking down of inhibitions regarding adultery
- The revolt of the youth against parents
- A rapid rise in juvenile delinquency
- The common acceptance of all forms of sexual perversion[9]

Dr. Carle Zimmerman wrote that in 1947! If we could assign numerical values to each of his points, we would have to multiply each one by several times to accurately portray where we are today.

If we don't provide the safeguards, the standards, and if we don't set up the fence posts and protective boundaries for our children, their world will do it for them, or they will do it themselves. The inevitable result will be that many will be led to despair and confusion and broken hearts and broken bodies and broken dreams. The idea is presented quite clearly in one modern translation of Proverbs 19:18: **Discipline your children while they are young enough to learn. If you don't, you are helping them destroy *themselves*** (GNT).

This leads me to a second timeless truth.

There Has Never Been a Better Time to Shepherd Our Children

Maybe you're tempted to think that practicing biblical discipline will bring disruption and chaos into your home.

Take it by faith, take in godly counsel, and take your time. Clearly communicate to your children the two or three or four actions that will bring about a spanking, and show them where God's Word has actually commanded you to discipline them.

Then patiently watch for what Solomon says to those who consistently apply biblical discipline in their home: **Correct your son, and he will give you comfort** (Proverbs 29:17). Many Bible versions translate that last word "peace." Contrary to popular opinion, biblical discipline does *not* bring chaos and turmoil but peace, comfort, and rest.

There has never been a better time than *now* to shepherd your children as a loving, authoritative parent. There has never been a more critical time to start teaching the truth, holding the standard, and lovingly disciplining your children.

May God give you the courage and faith to trust His Word enough to obey it . . . and to shepherd your children to do the same.

9

DANGEROUS AFFAIRS

Proverbs 5–7

On the night of February 7, 1996, Kevin left the bowling alley in Plant City, Florida, and picked up two friends in his white Camaro. Kevin's friend Brian was riding in the front passenger seat, and Randall was sitting in the back seat.

The three eighteen-year-olds thought they had the right of way as they drove through an intersection on Keysville Road. After all, there was no stop sign at the intersection. Unknown to them, the stop sign that *should* have been there had been taken down. A loaded semitrailer truck plowed into the Camaro, and all three young men in the car were killed instantly.

> Investigators say what took their lives was a prank, an act of vandalism by strangers. A stop sign that should have warned them of the cross-street ahead, a thoroughfare for long-haul truckers, had been deliberately knocked down.[1]

A quick search on the internet will demonstrate that stealing traffic signs is common and costly, and the favorite sign to steal is the stop sign. Just outside Tampa, Florida, it cost much more than money—it cost the lives of three young men.

Our world is in the process of removing another "stop sign." It's being removed with alarming speed and equally alarming results—the casualties are mounting.

Our culture has removed the stop signs whenever sexual issues are encountered and is replacing them with "Speed Up" signs or even "Congratulations for Not Stopping" signs.

Our world has now labeled sexual behavior outside of marriage as "alternative lifestyles" or "legal acts between consenting adults" or "rites of passage." Any thought of restraint is dismissed.

Our generation even likes to apply the word *safe* to sex outside of marriage. There's no such thing as safe sex outside of marriage. Declaring it "safe" is like going to an area along the ocean beach where sharks have been sighted and riptides observed and hammering up a sign that says, "Safe Swimming"; or going to the edge of a drainage ditch, next to an industrial plant and posting a sign that says, "Safe Drinking Water." Sin is *never* safe.

I have been challenged by the writing of a famous author who gave some powerful warnings about promiscuity and infidelity. It came out of his own home life.

This author had seen what sexual sin had done to his father. His dad had gotten involved with the wife of one of his employees. As the boss, he had pushed his weight around. Still, the woman willingly went along. Their one-night stand led to pregnancy, and when he heard the news, he became furious. He didn't want anyone to find out because it would ruin his reputation. So, he swore the woman to secrecy and then, without her knowledge, he had someone on his security detail make sure her husband didn't make it home from work alive. He later married the woman to further cover up the affair.

The famous author was this couple's second child . . . his name was Solomon.

As a young man, Solomon was troubled by stolen stop signs. His collection of proverbs put up new ones that read:

- Danger Ahead!
- Dead End!
- No Trespassing!
- Make a U-Turn!
- Stop!

Sexual sin is the *only* subject in Proverbs to which Solomon devotes two entire chapters, as well as portions of other chapters. Solomon will take us to the scene of one particular collision and illustrate his warning as graphically as he can in Proverbs chapter 5, part of chapter 6, and all of chapter 7.

WARNING ABOUT DANGEROUS AFFAIRS

It Starts with Delight

> **My son, give attention to my wisdom, incline your ear to my understanding; that you may observe discretion and your lips may reserve knowledge. For the lips of an adulteress drip honey and smoother than oil is her speech.** (Proverbs 5:1-3)

The word for **adulteress** might be translated in your version "strange woman." Solomon is simply using a word that refers to a woman who is "not related"; in other words, she isn't this man's wife. She will appear in chapters 6, 7, 22, and 23. Her speech is **smoother than oil**, Solomon writes here in verse 3.

In chapter 7, Solomon watches a man race toward an intersection, ignoring God's warning signs to stop!

> **For at the window of my house I looked out through my lattice, and I saw among the naive, and discerned among the youths a young man lacking sense, passing through the street near her corner; and he takes the way to her house, in the twilight, in the evening, in the middle of the night and in the darkness. And behold, a woman comes to meet him, dressed as a harlot and cunning of heart. She is boisterous and rebellious, her feet do not remain at home; she is now in the streets, now in the squares, and lurks by every corner. So she seizes him and kisses him and with a brazen face she says to him: "I was due to offer peace offerings; today I have paid my vows. Therefore I have come out to meet you, To seek your presence earnestly, and I have found you."** (verses 6-15)

The truth is, she really doesn't care who he is; he will only be used for her own sensual cravings, and quite frankly, he will use her for the same. This scenario implies that she already knows him.

She says further in verses 16-17, **"I have spread my couch with coverings, with colored linens of Egypt. I have sprinkled my bed with myrrh, aloes and cinnamon."**

This Egyptian linen actually refers to linens of red color, a luxury exported by ancient Egypt. Color was a sign of status, so she specifically mentions colored linens in verse 16. Furthermore, these perfumes had to be purchased from merchants who traveled great distances; because of that, perfumes like these were prized and even displayed as part of a king's treasury.[2]

This woman is portraying herself to this man as a queen. In other words, she's not some lowlife woman from the back alley. She's wealthy and sophisticated. She's even religious. She mentions that she's all caught up with her sacrifices and religious vows (verse 14).

She's not looking for just *anybody*. She's waited for *him*. She flatters away in verse 15, saying, **"I have come . . . to seek your presence earnestly."** She's saying, "*You* are the one worthy of my love!"

People involved in adultery have convinced themselves that they are worth more than their spouse can see in them and that only the person they are with is able to truly appreciate them. Ironically, the foundation for appreciation is integrity and trust and truth, and that means they have become involved in something that is destined for disappointment. There is a total absence of integrity, trust, and truth.

A study was conducted with men who had left their spouses for "the other woman." These men were interviewed ten years after their affair and the breakup of their home.

- 33 percent were intensely angry with life.
- 50 percent ended up divorced again, most of them from the woman they had believed was the answer to all their problems.
- 80 percent experienced the same or lower quality of life financially.
- 50 percent under the age of fifty were unhappily remarried.
- 66 percent over the age of fifty were unhappily remarried.
- 80 percent [!] of these men would remarry their former wives and regain what they lost if given the chance.[3]

What begins with delight soon reaches the next stage.

Delight Turns to Disgust

Solomon writes in Proverbs 5, verses 3-4: **For the lips of an adulteress drip honey and smoother than oil is her speech; but in the end she is bitter as wormwood, sharp as a two-edged sword.** In other words, the taste of honey is soon replaced with the taste of wormwood, a plant in Palestine from which a bitter drink was made. Jealousy, disrespect, betrayal, and guilt quickly displace the initial feelings of excitement.

Commenting on this text, Warren Wiersbe wrote, "Solomon is suggesting that a wise person checks out the destination before buying a ticket."[4]

Disgust Digresses to Dishonor

> **Keep your way far from her and do not go near the door of her house, or you will give your vigor to others and your years to the cruel one; and strangers will be filled with your strength and your hard-earned goods will go to the house of an alien.** (Proverbs 5:8-10)

What a perfect description of alimony and the frustration brought about by sin. Perhaps it's not even your sin. Perhaps in your case it's your spouse's sin that now pulls your hard-earned money into somebody else's bank account. If so, remember that one day God will finish the books and settle the score. In the meantime, keep trusting Him and doing what's right.

But to someone *considering* adultery, Solomon writes in Proverbs 6:27, **Can a man take fire in his bosom and his clothes not be burned?** That's another way of saying, "If you play with fire, you *will* get burned."

In verse 33, Solomon warns further, **Wounds and disgrace he will find, and his reproach will not be blotted out**. In other words, though confession and forgiveness are always possible for the truly repentant, the consequences will be felt for a lifetime. Adam and Eve were forgiven, but they were expelled from the garden.

The man or woman driving toward that intersection with immorality might see street signs marked "Freedom," "Excitement," "Acceptance," or "Gratification," but Solomon plants a sign that says, "Disaster Ahead."

These are dangerous affairs. They may start with delight, but they soon turn to disgust and dishonor.

Dishonor Leads to Disaster

Solomon continues in Proverbs 5:11: **And you groan at your final end, when your flesh and your body are consumed.** Solomon is describing the effects of sexually transmitted diseases.

This is the part that isn't going to make it into the movies. This isn't in the tabloids. It's not in the movie trailer when the guy finally gets the woman and they give way to their passions.

But Solomon isn't writing for a box-office hit. He's not producing a thirty-second commercial; he's telling the truth.

Sexual sin brings a harvest of decay and loss. And Solomon highlights several losses. In verse 11, he speaks of the loss of health, as **your flesh and your body are consumed**. In our age of so-called safe sex, the media is virtually silent on the epidemic of sexually transmitted diseases, not to mention the physical and emotional effects of guilt and betrayal and despair.

According to a report from the Centers for Disease Control and Prevention, there were 26 million new cases of sexually transmitted infections in the United States in 2018, bringing the total at the time to nearly 68 million, or 20 percent of the population.[5] These include hepatitis B and Syphilis, as well as genital herpes and HIV/AIDS, for which there are no cure.

We live in a culture that would rather remove the stop signs and enjoy sin for a season than subject themselves to the moral law of God, even if it means paying a physical price later.

Health *and* wealth are impacted by adultery and immorality in general. One study found that 73 percent of the women who left their spouses for another man, reported experiencing a lower standard of living.[6]

We don't have time to delve into all the possible losses incurred by sexual immorality, but Proverbs 5–7 catalogues some of them:

- Loss of security
- Loss of friendships
- Loss of trust
- Loss of reputation
- Loss of peace
- Loss of fellowship with God

The most expensive, destructive, dangerous thing in the world is *immorality*. Frankly, immorality is insanity!

Disaster Leads to Despair

The last stage in this downward spiral is despair. Listen to the despair coming from the lips of someone who now knows the tragic consequences of his dangerous affairs:

> **"How I have hated instruction! And my heart spurned reproof! I have not listened to the voice of my teachers, nor inclined my ear to my instructors! I was almost in utter ruin in the midst of the assembly and congregation."** (Proverbs 5:12-14)

This person is part of God's assembly—he is in the midst of God's people. He's a prodigal who is now wishing he had never left home. He's lamenting, "How I hated instruction and reproof. I hated *the stop signs* from God."

Solomon ends his warning about dangerous affairs in chapter 7:

> **Now therefore, my sons, listen to me, and pay attention to the words of my mouth. Do not let your heart turn aside to her ways, do not stray into her paths. For many are the victims she has cast down, and numerous are all her slain.** (verses 24-26)

I remember watching an interview on a major network of a woman who ran an adult internet site. She said with a great deal of pride that the men who visited her site were men who probably never went beyond their moral boundaries before the internet came along. She estimated at the time that 600,000 men had visited her website.

AVOIDING DANGEROUS AFFAIRS

Solomon could not make the dangers of sexual sin any clearer. It must be avoided! So, what practical precautions can we take to avoid it? Here are five.

Don't Justify Little Compromises as Innocent

Dangerous affairs do not begin in the bedroom. They begin in the boardroom, in the classroom, at the baseball field, in the gym, or at your local YMCA. They find a home in the heart before they act out in the flesh.

Don't Wait until Temptation Is upon You to Make Your Battle Plan

Plan ahead. Fight the skirmishes early in your mind. The best place to apply the brakes and stop is early on. As I recall, an old Puritan writer put it this way: "Pour godly thoughts on the hot coals of desire." You're already in danger if you've begun making excuses.

Don't Assume You Are above or beyond Any Temptation

Never allow yourself to say or think things like these:

- "Nothing like that will happen to me."
- "That's not a problem for me."
- "Something like this isn't all that wrong."
- "I can stop whenever I want."

Don't fool yourself into believing what I have heard people say: "We're not hurting anybody." Oh, yes, you are. There is a financial cost, a physical cost, an emotional cost, a spiritual cost, a character cost, and a future cost to sin. Sin always has a cost, and it is more than we can imagine.

It is often said that sin will take you farther than you want to go, keep you longer than you want to stay, and cost you more than you want to pay.

Stay Away from Any Place Where You Would Not Want to Be Seen

Listen to that voice that whispers, "You don't belong here; this party isn't where you want to be. This internet site or chat room isn't where you should be. You don't want to be seen here." Consider this voice of conscience God's warning signal to run!

Be Honest when Temptation Knocks, and Ask Christ to Answer the Door

The power of temptation rests in the pleasure temptation promises. If stolen waters weren't sweet (Proverbs 9:17), no one would steal the water.[7]

The enemy of your soul knows that Jesus Christ now lives in the apartment of your heart. But he still sends people to your door, wanting you to come out and play. They show up like the pizza delivery guy who comes to your house by accident at 8:00 p.m. when you're in the middle of that diet.

In the world of real, spiritual temptation, send your Lord to answer the door. Let Him respond to all the calls of temptation. Say, "Lord, you need to respond because I can't. Spirit of God, intervene here because I'm weak."

Stay Alert at All Times

If I had a nickel for every time I told my kids when they were driving home at night to watch out for deer, I would be rich. There are a lot of deer in the area where we live, and we often see deer that have been hit by cars. Whenever our children called and said, "We're on our way home." I would say, "Watch out for deer—it's getting late."

One day I dropped my daughter off at school at 8:00 a.m. and pulled out onto the highway. I got up to forty-five miles per hour, and suddenly, out of nowhere, a deer ran in front of me—and wham! That doe rolled over two or three times—instantly killed—and the front of my pickup truck splintered and scattered everywhere.

My kids? They never once hit a deer, and here I collided with one in broad daylight! Deer aren't supposed to be out in broad daylight. They're supposed to be in the woods, taking care of Bambi or talking to Thumper, not running around on a highway.

But that's where I went wrong. I had assumed *when* deer would pose a danger to me—and they certainly wouldn't be a problem at 8:30 in the morning.

You won't believe how alert I am now . . . at 8:30 in the morning.

- Don't justify little compromises as innocent.
- Don't wait until temptation is upon you to make your battle plan.
- Don't assume you are above or beyond any temptation.

- Stay away from any place where you would not want to be caught or seen.
- Be honest when temptation knocks, and ask Christ to answer the door.
- Stay alert at all times.

While you're at it, don't take stop signs down where God has put them up. He put them up for a reason—for your health and hope and joy and progress and safety. Leave them alone. And daily ask the Lord to help you pay attention every time you see one along the roadway of your life.

10

FACING THE MUSIC

Proverbs 6:16-19

Robert Jeffress included in his book on Proverbs an interesting story, which according to some, explains the origin of a popular phrase we often use today.

> A number of years ago a man talked his way into playing in an orchestra, although he had no musical training. Whenever the orchestra would practice or perform, he would hold his flute against his lips and pretend to play. He received a salary from the orchestra and enjoyed a relatively affluent lifestyle. One day, however, the emperor of China requested a solo from each musician in the orchestra. The flutist became nervous. There was no way he could master the instrument in such a short amount of time. He feigned illness, but the emperor's physician could not be fooled. On the day of his scheduled performance, the imposter drank poison and killed himself. His experience led to the common expression, "He refused to face the music."[1]

As used today, the expression "face the music" means to take responsibility for one's actions and accept the consequences. It means to be accountable, to own up to what one is and has done.

If you study the book of Proverbs very long, you will get the distinct impression that the Emperor of heaven has called each of us in for a personal evaluation, and there's no hiding our performance. In fact, it's impossible to escape Him in life or in death.

Perhaps that's why the apostle Paul was so passionate about his service for the glory of God. He wrote, "We also have as our ambition . . . to be pleasing to Him [Christ]" (2 Corinthians 5:9).

The hard truth is that we're often not very pleasing to our Lord. We're in constant need of challenge and correction.

One of the greatest dangers to our growth in Christ is adopting the arrogant yet subtle belief that we have already arrived. Paul countered this idea with his own humble words: "Not that I have already . . . become perfect [or fully mature], but I press on" (Philippians 3:12).

It is a good practice to periodically "face the music" by allowing Scripture to evaluate us and expose us for who we really are and where we're really at spiritually.

In Proverbs 6:16-19 God calls us in for a personal evaluation by the Emperor:

> **There are six things which the LORD hates, yes, seven which are an abomination to Him: Haughty eyes, a lying tongue, and hands that shed innocent blood, a heart that devises wicked plans, feet that run rapidly to evil, a false witness who utters lies, and one who spreads strife among brothers.**

This passage might be more like getting a physical from the Divine Physician. Notice that most of the sinful activities in this list are associated with parts of the body. He refers to the eyes and speaks of the plans of the heart and the use of the tongue, the hands, and the feet.

Now if you have a particularly good doctor, he (or she) will tell you, not only what to do, but also what to *stop* doing. He will tell you some things you need to start practicing and some things you need to start eating, and he will also tell you what to stop eating. He's such a nosey person!

In the same way, our Divine Physician personally examines us, providing an honest diagnosis of our condition. He tells us exactly what we need to know.

WHY A LIST OF SEVEN SINS?

Before we look at each of the sins in Solomon's list in Proverbs 6:16-19, let's consider why he gives us this poetic list of seven.

It Aids the Believer with His Memory

My wife will occasionally say, "Honey, while you're out, will you stop at the grocery store and pick up a couple of things?" Now, if it really is just a couple of things, I can remember them. But if it's more than a couple of things, I'm likely to forget something. I will end up arriving home with white-powdered doughnuts and diet granola bars, which in my view cancel one another out. So, I write out a list of the things I need to get.

Now, if my grocery list is brief and written in poetic form, as Solomon's list is, I might not even need to refer to it as I walk the grocery aisles. Solomon's list of seven sins, then, is designed to be easily memorized.

It Encourages the Believer by Its Brevity

Certainly, the Lord hates all sin, and all sin is equally hated by God. But to summarize and thus pare down so many sins into a short list of seven encourages the believer. Imagine if the text said, "There are six thousand things the Lord hates, actually seven thousand that are an abomination to Him."

Seven thousand? We will never please Him! So, let's focus on these seven.

It Surprises the Believer with Its Severity

These seven sins, Solomon says, **the LORD hates**. The Lord despises these actions and attitudes, calling them together an **abomination**! That word means "morally repulsive."[2]

Does this mean the Lord considers these seven sins more repulsive than all other sins? No, for *all* sin is an abomination to God. In fact, the wording, **six things . . . yes, seven**, is simply a Hebrew expression that implies the list is not exhaustive.[3]

Sin is sin. However, some of the sins listed here are surprising. We might even be tempted to sweep them under the rug! They seem like a far cry from the dirty dozen or the nasty nine.

We understand the repulsiveness of shedding **innocent blood**—that's murder. But we might be tempted to say, "God hates arrogance, or **haughty eyes**, as much as He hates murder?" Yes.

Listen to the Physician's report. "The Lord hates murder and lying and divisiveness and arrogance *equally*."

WHAT GOD HATES

Let's face the music together. This is what God says in verse 16: **There are six things which the LORD hates, yes, seven which are an abomination to Him**.

A Disdainful Spirit

The Divine Physician begins His list with **haughty eyes**. In our vernacular we might call this "looking down your nose at everybody else." This speaks of an attitude that literally disdains others.

The eyes serve as the mirror of the soul, which means this haughty look betrays a haughty spirit.[4] People with **haughty eyes** act as if they are better than other people because they believe they *are*.

This is the attitude of Satan, who disdained the triune God, believing he was worthy of God's own throne. The person who views others with arrogance is reflecting the spirit of Satan, and this spirit will never bring glory to Christ.

The Scottish preacher James Denney said, "No man can bear witness to Christ and to himself at the same time."[5] In other words, you can't be impressed with Christ and at the same time be impressed with yourself.

This phrase refers to people who are conceited—whose favorite topic of conversation is themselves.

I appreciate Walt Disney's response years ago when someone asked him what it was like to be a celebrity. He said:

> As far as I can remember, being a celebrity has never helped me make a good picture . . . or command the obedience of my daughter, or impress my wife. It doesn't even seem to help keep fleas off our dog, and if being a celebrity won't give one an advantage over a couple of fleas, then I guess there can't be that much in being a celebrity after all.[6]

A Deceitful Spirit

Verse 17 lists a second thing the Lord hates: **a lying tongue**. Again, this mirrors the character of Satan, whom Christ calls the Father of lies. In fact, whenever Satan speaks, he speaks in his native tongue—the dialect of lying (John 8:44).

Jesus Christ, on the other hand, always speaks the truth. In fact, He identifies Himself *as* the truth (John 14:6).

The believer who is most like Christ and most unlike Satan is the one who consistently tells the truth. Over and over again, Solomon challenges the believer to be honest. He writes in Proverbs 4:24, "Put away from you a deceitful mouth and put devious speech far from you."

Devious speech isn't just some big whopper of a lie. It could be manipulating the truth to cover your tracks, flattery to get your way, or stretching the truth to fit your story.[7]

A Destructive Spirit

Solomon now informs us that the Lord is examining, not just the eyes and the tongue, but also the **hands that shed innocent blood**. We would certainly expect to find this on a list of seven terrible sins.

This describes the murderers and the fomenters of holocausts and genocide. But it also includes the euthanasia proponent and the abortionist. This includes all those who adopt the message of Peter Singer, the bioethicist at Princeton who argued that killing both preborn and newborn children, as well as assisted suicide, especially for the elderly, is acceptable if it is within the best interests of the family.

Singer said in an interview a number of years ago that he believes "the next few decades will see a massive upheaval in the concept of life and rights, with only 'a rump of hard-core, know-nothing religious fundamentalists' still protecting life as [sacred]." He believes that killing a disabled newborn for up to twenty-eight days after birth is acceptable and that "man's life is not worth more than . . . a cow."[8]

Singer has a growing following. A man in our church who has a son with Down syndrome and testifies to the delight and blessing his son has been in his family sent me a local news article more than a dozen years ago. It quoted a university biology professor's comment to a class that a mother who discovers her preborn child has Down syndrome should abort it. He said it's "the moral thing to do."[9]

The Word of God is clear: The Lord *hates* that perspective. He hates the industry of death that determines who is valuable and worthy of life and who is not.

Many today have been deceived into following this line of thinking by Satan, the god of this world, who is bent on deception and destruction. "He was a murderer from the beginning," Christ says in John 8:44.

Satan is also called the "great red dragon" in Revelation 12:3, probably given this name because of his thirst for the shedding of blood. He cannot kill God, whom he hates, but he motivates and inspires the killing of human beings because we are uniquely created in the image of God.

A Depraved Spirit

Solomon writes in verse 18 that the Lord hates **a heart that devises wicked plans**. This text refers to those who are plotting to take advantage of others.[10] They have a depraved spirit, always conniving, scheming, and scamming others (see Proverbs 24:8).

If the world is full of scammers and schemers who seek to steal our money and our purity and our reputation, let the church be an assembly that purposely and carefully plans to enrich our walk and encourage our purity and enhance our character and reputation.

Howard Hendricks once wrote:

> Not long ago I lost one of my best friends, a woman eighty-six years old. . . .
>
> The last time I saw her on planet Earth was at one of those aseptic Christian parties. We were sitting there on egg-shells, looking pious, when she walked in and said, "Well, Hendricks, I haven't seen you for a long time. What are the five best books you've read in the past year?"
>
> She had a way of changing a group's dynamics. Her philosophy was, Let's not bore each other with each other; let's get

> into a discussion, and if we can't find anything to discuss, let's get into an argument.
>
> She was eighty-three on her last trip to the Holy Land. She went there with a group of NFL football players. One of my most vivid memories of her is seeing her out front yelling back to them, "Come on men, get with it!"
>
> She died in her sleep . . . Her daughter told me that just before she died, she had written out her goals for the next ten years.[11]

Now that's a heart devising plans for good.

A Delinquent Spirit

Continuing in verse 18, Solomon moves on to the feet. He informs us that the Lord hates **feet that run rapidly to evil**. These are wandering feet, which speak of a delinquent spirit.

Solomon is describing people who just have the ability to find trouble. They have the innate skill to sniff the wind and discover which direction sin is in, and then, with both feet, run as fast as they can toward it. They are not discovered *by* evil; they long for evil; they *live* for evil.

This is the high school senior who has already decided that as soon as he's away from home in college somewhere, he will run to evil. This is the businessman whose flight touches down in a distant city, and his feet are anxious to start searching for sin.

God hates the sound of feet running with delight away from His pleasure and into the arms of sin. He longs for the sound of the prodigal whose feet race toward home.

A Dishonest Spirit

Solomon writes in verse 19 that the Lord hates **a false witness who utters lies.** He also penned Proverbs 19:22: "It is better to be a poor man than a liar."

Apply that in your business dealings next week. Will you lie and get the contract or tell the truth and lose the deal?

In Proverbs 26:28, Solomon writes, "A lying tongue hates those it crushes, and a flattering mouth works ruin." Neither the liar nor the flatterer tells the truth, and both will ruin lives. Sadly, Solomon's own son, Rehoboam, would see his kingdom torn apart because he listened to counselors who flattered him and puffed up his pride and caused him to make foolish decisions (1 Kings 12).

Proverbs 6:19 particularly has in view a person who is called to take the witness stand and deliver true testimony. The one who doesn't tell the truth brings dishonor upon the accused and is performing an act hated by God.

The need to assure truthful testimony led to the tradition of witnesses placing their hands on the Bible before they took the witness stand and promising to tell the truth, the whole truth, and nothing but the truth, adding, "So help me God."

The believer is always to tell the truth, the whole truth, and nothing but the truth. The Christian is *always* under oath!

A Divisive Spirit

Proverbs 6:19 concludes with the seventh thing God hates: **one who spreads strife among brothers.** He hates anyone and anything that creates dissension and separates His saints.

We can either sow the seeds that bring a harvest of blessing (Psalm 126:5-6), or we can sow slander, which brings a harvest of bitter hurt.

WHAT GOD LOVES

If God hates these seven sins, then He must love their opposites. So, let's turn around these seven deadly sins and consider seven delightful acts.[12] These are the things the Lord loves.

- Instead of a haughty spirit, demonstrate *a humble spirit.* Will you look *down* on people or look *out* for people?
- Instead of lying speech, pursue *truthful speech.* Tell the truth—in big things and small things.
- Instead of hands that harm, develop *hands that help.*
- Instead of a heart that plans wicked deeds, develop a heart that plans *wholesome deeds.*

- Instead of racing toward evil, race to *do good*—run for the prize of the high calling you have in Christ Jesus (Philippians 3:14).
- Instead of lying, live before the Lord as an *honest witness*. Remember, you are under oath.
- Instead of sowing bitterness and disunity, sow seeds of *blessing and unity*.

In doing these things, you are mirroring the character and actions of Christ.

- He was the model of humility.
- He was the epitome of truth and truthfulness.
- His hands healed, helped, and embraced.
- His heart was pure and sinless.
- His feet walked among us, showing us what it means to pursue what is good.
- Everything He said was the truth and nothing but the truth.
- His Spirit has unified us around the truth.

Face up to the music . . . take in the Divine Physician's report. Let's accept the diagnosis, not argue with the x-rays or the lab report. Let's fill the prescription and take our medicine.

And with gratitude for God's grace, let's yield our eyes, mouth, hands, heart, and feet—everything we are—to Him.

ENDNOTES

CHAPTER ONE

[1] Andrea Aker, "Two Stashes of Gold Loot Remain a Mystery Near Flagstaff," Arizona Oddities, June 7, 2013, arizonaoddities.com.

[2] Ze'ev Yeivin, "The Mysterious Silver Hoard from Eshtemoa," *Biblical Archaeology Review* 13:06 (November-December 1987), 38-44.

[3] This illustration has been adapted from Robert Jeffress, *The Solomon Secrets* (Waterbrook Press, 2002), 9.

[4] Warren W. Wiersbe, *Be Skillful: Proverbs* (Victor Books, 1995), 21.

[5] Jeffress, 8.

[6] John Phillips, *Exploring Proverbs, Volume One: An Expository Commentary* (Kregel, 1995), 18.

[7] Ray Pritchard, *The ABC'S of Wisdom* (Moody Press, 1997), 62.

[8] Ed Young, *Been There, Done That: Now What?* (Broadman & Holman, 1994), 29.

CHAPTER TWO

[1] Derek Kidner, *The Proverbs: An Introduction and Commentary* (Inter-Varsity Press, 1964), 35.

[2] Warren W. Wiersbe, *Be Skillful: Proverbs* (Victor Books, 1995), 7.

[3] John Phillips, *Exploring Proverbs, Volume One: An Expository Commentary* (Kregel, 1995), 14.

[4] Wiersbe, 14.

[5] Ibid., 13.

[6] Richard L. Mayhue, *Practicing Proverbs* (Christian Focus, 2000), 41.

[7] Derek Leman, *Proverbial Wisdom & Common Sense* (Lederer Books, 1999), 11.

[8] Josh McDowell, *Right from Wrong* (Word Publishing, 1994), 6.

[9] Ibid., 10.

[10] Leman, 12.

[11] "Planetary Alignment Decreases Gravity," Museum of Hoaxes, hoaxes.com.

[12] Bruce K. Waltke, *The Book of Proverbs: Chapters 1–15* (Eerdmans, 2004), 178.

[13] See, for example, "Oedipus the King," *History Today* 69:9, September 9, 2019, historytoday.com.

CHAPTER THREE

[1] Haddon W. Robinson, "Foreword" in Robert L. Alden, *Proverbs: A Commentary on an Ancient Book of Timeless Advice* (Baker, 1983), 7.

[2] Ibid.

[3] Ibid.

[4] "More Intelligence-Challenged People," Haven on Earth, "Smile Pages," a-haven-on-earth.com.

[5] Peter A. Stevenson, *A Commentary on Proverbs* (BJU Press, 2001), 9.

[6] See Bruce K. Waltke, *The Book of Proverbs: Chapters 1–15* (Eerdmans, 2004), 100.

[7] Alden, *Proverbs*, 22.

[8] Chuck Yeager, *Yeager: An Autobiography* (Bantam, 986), 234-35. Note that ailerons are hinged surfaces on the back edges of the wings that control the aircraft in rolls, or banking.

CHAPTER FOUR

[1] C. S. Lewis, *The Four Loves* (HarperCollins, 1960), 103.

[2] Bruce K. Waltke, *The Book of Proverbs: Chapters 1–15* (Eerdmans, 2004), 190.

[3] Ibid., 571.

CHAPTER FIVE

[1] Fritz Rienecker and Cleon Rogers, *Linguistic Key to the Greek New Testament* (Regency, 1980), 582.

[2] Bruce K. Waltke, *The Book of Proverbs: Chapters 1–15* (Eerdmans, 2004), 476.

[3] Charles Swindoll, *Selected Studies from Proverbs* (IFL, 1994), 52.

[4] Ray Pritchard, *The ABC'S of Wisdom* (Moody Press, 1997), 477.

[5] Peter A. Stevenson, *A Commentary on Proverbs* (BJU Press, 2001), 292.

[6] Ibid., 367.

[7] Waltke, 339.

[8] "Incredible Insects of the Rain Forest," Kid Explorers, christiananswers.net.

[9] "How Strong Are Ants?" Ants.com.

[10] "Leafcutter Ant," *Encyclopaedia Britannica*, britannica.com.

[11] "Red Fire Ants," pests.org.

[12] Dana Stephens, "Kids of the Kingdom," *Christian Reader* (July/August 2000).

[13] See Waltke, 337, for the word meanings here.

[14] "Riggers Pledge," parachuteservices.com.

CHAPTER SIX

[1] *Bring Home the Bacon and Cutting the Mustard: The Origins and Meaning of the Food We Speak* (Castle Books, 2002), 81.

[2] Robert J. Morgan, *Nelson's Complete Book of Illustrations* (Thomas Nelson, 2000), 261.

[3] John Phillips, *Exploring Proverbs, Volume One: An Expository Commentary* (Kregel, 1995), 518.

[4] John Phillips, *Exploring Proverbs, Volume Two: An Expository Commentary* (Kregel, 1996), 393-94.

[5] Charles Bridges, *Proverbs* (Mott Media, 1978), 553.

[6] Max Lucado, *Facing Your Giants* (W Publishing Group, 2006), 65.

[7] Phillips, *Exploring Proverbs, Volume Two*, 550.

[8] Ray Pritchard, *The ABC'S of Wisdom* (Moody Press, 1997), 290.

CHAPTER SEVEN

[1] See Alice Gray, compiler, *Stories for the Heart* (Multnomah, 1996), 97; and "Lawnchair Larry Flight," wikipedia.org.

[2] Bruce K. Waltke, *The Book of Proverbs: Chapters 1–15* (Eerdmans, 2004), 277.

[3] Taken from Stuart Hample and Eric Marshall, compilers, *Children's Letters to God* (Workman Publishing, 1991).

[4] Waltke, 277.

[5] Charlie W. Shedd, *Letters to Philip on How to Treat a Woman* (Revel, 1970), 38.

CHAPTER EIGHT

[1] Tedd Tripp, *Shepherding a Child's Heart*, revised edition (Shepherd Press, 2005).

[2] Ginger Plowman, *Don't Make Me Count to Three* (Shepherd Press, 2003).

[3] Charles R. Swindoll, *Family Life* (Multnomah Press, 1988).

[4] Ibid., 102.

[5] Tripp, 4.

[6] Ibid.

[7] Ibid.

[8] Chart adapted from Swindoll, 113.

[9] Cited in Swindoll, 33.

CHAPTER NINE

[1] Sue Carlton, "Missing Road Sign Spins Long Legacy of Misery," *Tampa Bay Times*, October 1, 2005, tampabay.com.

[2] Bruce K. Waltke, *The Book of Proverbs: Chapters 1–15* (Eerdmans, 2004), 374.

[3] Cited in Robert Jeffress, *The Solomon Secrets* (Waterbrook Press, 2002), 119.

[4] Warren W. Wiersbe, *Be Skillful: Proverbs* (Victor Books, 1995), 49.

[5] "Sexually Transmitted Infections Prevalence, Incidence, and Cost Estimates in the United States," Centers for Disease Control and Prevention, published January 2021, cdc.gov.

[6] Cited in Jeffress, 118.

[7] Ibid., 114.

CHAPTER TEN

[1] Robert Jeffress, *The Solomon Secrets* (Waterbrook Press, 2002), 128.

[2] Peter A. Stevenson, *A Commentary on Proverbs* (BJU Press, 2001), 84.

[3] John Phillips, *Exploring Proverbs, Volume One: An Expository Commentary* (Kregel, 1995), 145.

[4] Stevenson, 84.

[5] Cited in Warren W. Wiersbe, *Be Skillful: Proverbs* (Victor Books, 1995), 155.

[6] Stephen Arterburn and Bill Farrel, *The One Year Book of Devotions for Men on the Go* (Tyndale House, 2004), 162.

[7] Jeffress, 126.

[8] "'Bioethicist': OK to Kill Babies after They're Born," WorldNetDaily, worldnetdaily.com, September 14, 2006.

[9] Samuel Spies, "UNC Prof Wary of Down Syndrome," Raleigh *News and Observer*, February 16, 2008, B1.

[10] Stevenson, 84.

[11] Howard Hendricks, *Teaching to Change Lives* (Multnomah Books, 1987), 23.

[12] As suggested by Allen P. Ross, "Proverbs," in *The Expositor's Bible Commentary*, ed. Frank E. Gaebelein, vol. 5 (Zondervan, 1991), 936.